Transforming Feminism

Maria Riley, OP

Sheed & Ward

G

Copyright© 1989
Center of Concern
Washington, DC

Sheed & Ward™ is a service of National Catholic Reporter Publishing
Company, Inc.

Library of Congress Catalog Card Number: 89-60583

ISBN: 1-55612-270-5

Published by: Sheed & Ward
               115 E. Armour Blvd., P.O. Box 419492
               Kansas City, MO 64141-6492

To order, call: (800) 333-7373

To my Adrian Dominican Sisters
who have supported and called me
to live my own truth
as a woman
as a Catholic

and

To my colleagues at the Center of Concern
who, over the years, have challenged me
to re-think and refine that truth
every step of my way.

v

Contents

Acknowledgments

No book is the work of one person. It results from a cumulative process of shared ideas and insights, absorbed, developed, and tempered over years. This book has been nurtured in the feminist community, in the justice and peace community, and in a large community of women who would not necessarily call themselves feminists, such as my sister Mary Jane Ryan. I have tried to be faithful to the voices I have heard and the yearnings I have shared. But I have also struggled to be faithful to my own truth. It has not always been easy.

In particular I want to acknowledge the group of feminist scholars in Washington, DC, who have faithfully read and commented on several different drafts of this manuscript: Jane Blewett, Cheryl Clemons, Ann Clifford, CSJ, Mary Collins, OSB, Sarah Fahy, SND, Mary Hines, SND, Mary Irving, SSND, Helen J. John, SND, Elizabeth Johnson, CSJ, Georgia Keightley, Margaret Mary Kelleher, OSU, Sally Ann McReynolds, SND, Patricia Parachini, SNJM, and Catherine Vincie, RSHM.

My colleagues at the Center of Concern have supported me in multiple ways throughout this work. I want to thank in particular Sylvia Diss, Peter Henriot, SJ, Anne Hope, Phil Land, SJ, Judy Mladineo, George Ann Potter, Theresa Serene, and Candy Warner for their careful reading and thoughtful comments on the manuscript. James Hug, SJ, provided the last meticulous reading that brought the text to its final form. David Simmons, Lance Hinds, Andrea Pi-Sunyer, and Lucien Chauvin graciously provided technical assistance. I am grateful to them for their help in developing this work, but even more so, for their continuing encouragement of my work for the promotion of women.

Three members of my Adrian community reviewed the text and offered important contributions: Nadine Foley, OP, Attracta Kelly, OP, and Patricia Siemen, OP. I believe they will discover many traces of Adrian influence throughout the book.

They were nothing more than people, by themselves. Even paired, any pairing, they would have been nothing more than people by themselves. But all together, they have become the heart and muscles and mind of something perilous and new, something strange and growing and great.

Together, all together, they are the instruments of change.

The Bone People
Keri Hulme

Introduction

> . . . be patient toward all that is unsolved in your heart and [to] try
> to love the *questions themselves* . . . the point is, to live every-
> thing. *Live* the questions now. Perhaps you will then gradually,
> without noticing it, live along some distant day into the answer.
>
> —Rainer Maria Rilke[1]

"Why are you writing this book?" This question was posed by one of
the women in the feminist theological reflection group I am part of. We
often assist each other by reviewing and critiquing our "work in progress."
The question was so simple and yet so relevant to the evolution of this
work that I decided to answer it, first for myself and then for anyone who
may pick up this book either out of curiosity or personal search.

This book is part of my search as a Catholic feminist[2] for a perspective
and agenda for human liberation that brings together the two most
profound influences in my life: feminism and my Catholic faith as it is
lived by that community of believers who call themselves the People of
God. I do not believe these two influences are inimical. In more positive
terms, I believe in the potential of both these social forces to be mutually
transforming as well as to contribute to the transformation of those structures in both the church and the society that deny people the full experience of their humanity.

In the process of my search I have become more and more convinced
that "womenspirit rising" is one of the most far-reaching social revolutions
of our age, touching all dimensions of our lives, from personal identity to
our most intimate relationships, to the shape of our social and ecclesial institutions, to the content of our systems of human knowledge. It has raised
questions for which there are no ready answers. Its focus is not only justice for women, it is also about the shape of the future.

In working for justice for women in church and society, I found myself
more and more seeking to understand the implications of the changes that

are occurring and what kind of future they are shaping, socially, economically, politically, and culturally. For example, for the past two decades women have been entering the labor market at a rate of over 1.2 million a year. By 1986, 64% of all women under 65 years of age were employed, making up 44% of the paid work force.[3] This reality is changing patterns of relationships between women and men, creating new patterns of family life, adjusting the economic equation between women and men, diminishing the pool of women available for traditional volunteer work, and enlarging women's expectations for themselves.

These realities demand not only new social attitudes and policies, they also demand new social structures. They are making new claims on traditional social systems—governments, schools, families, churches, synagogues, social services, businesses.[4] They have also opened new horizons for social ethics as the profound but subtle shifting of social institutions has become evident.

This horizon where the women's movement and social structures meet led me to re-look at Catholic social thought and its contributions to shaping a just social order. In the process I found my feminist consciousness in dialogue with my Catholic social consciousness. I also realized how mutually transforming of both feminist thought and Catholic social thought the dialogue became in my search for a *Transforming Feminism*. The title intends to convey a double meaning: both the power of feminism to transform human relationships, social structures, and systems of thought as well as the continuing need of feminism to be transformed by the new insights and situations it encounters in its continuing quest for a more just world.

This book is an invitation to the readers to engage in the dialogue between feminist thought and Catholic social thought in their search for a feminism that holds promise for true human liberation both in the church and in the society. The chapters that follow situate the search within an understanding of the history and ideologies of contemporary feminism and an understanding of Catholic social thought. The wisdom of both feminist and liberation theology tells us that all insight and change come through personal experience. Honoring that wisdom, I begin Chapter One with personal experience—the story of my feminist search for liberation and an invitation to the reader to reflect upon her/his personal experience. Chapter Two situates these personal histories within the larger history of the women's movement in the U.S. during the late twentieth century. In Chapter Three, I introduce the process of feminist analysis and analyze the dominant ideologies of contemporary feminism: liberal, cultural, radical and socialist. Chapter Four introduces the main outlines of Catholic social thought. In this chapter, I also offer a feminist critique of Catholic social thought with a view to developing a feminist revision of it. The final chapter looks to the future. Each chapter invites the reader to engage in her/his own dialogue with feminism and with Catholic social thought.

The purpose of beginning a feminist revision of Catholic social thought is multiple. It could provide Catholic women and men with a perspective to bring to the wider feminist dialogue for social change. This perspective has been notably lacking within the feminist dialogue. It will also provide a corrective and enrichment of Catholic social thought by including the dimension of gender. Finally, a feminist-revised Catholic social ethic could be a powerful ally in women's struggle for human liberation.

I cannot end this introduction without admitting the inherent problem of raising the idea of Catholic social thought within a feminist context. The institutional patriarchy of the Roman Catholic church remains a stumbling block to any significant Catholic-feminist dialogue. It has also bred a subliminal anti-Catholicism within some feminist circles. Moreover, the patriarchy of the institutional church remains a central problem for Catholic feminists. Indeed, the history of the Church has long legitimated the cultural and social norms of discrimination against women. The frustration of many women within the church is great—so great that for some the only answer has been to leave the church.

For Catholic feminists who choose to remain within the faith tradition, the transformation of the church beyond patriarchy is the enduring agenda. Most of our writings and strategies have been aimed at revealing and transforming the patriarchy of the church as it takes shape in its all-male hierarchy, in its God-language and imagery, its sacramental life, its anthropology, its articulation of a male-defined theological, scriptural, and moral magisterial, and its subtle but all-pervasive misogyny. Catholic feminist scholars have brought a feminist critique to scripture studies, systematic theology, sexual ethics, church history, Mariology, liturgy; all of which is aimed at breaking open the entrenched patriarchy in the life and teaching of the church.

However, in this book I am not focusing primarily on the church. I am attempting to situate a feminist revision of Catholic social thought within the context of the larger society of which the church is a part. If my thesis —that feminism and Catholic social thought are mutually enriching and can empower us for the process of social transformation—has merit, then that transformation would perforce include both church and social structures.

Finally, my emphasis on Catholic social thought is not intended to exclude the contributions of other faith traditions. Each has a richness of insight to offer as well as an entrenched patriarchy to overcome. Rather, my emphasis on Catholic social thought is an attempt to carve out a perspective that is coherent with my own faith tradition. It is out of that perspective that I can enter into dialogue with other perspectives as we search together for a more just and peace-filled world. I invite feminists of other faiths to appropriate the social theology of their traditions in our mutual search for justice for women and men, the young and the old, the peoples of all nations and races, and for the earth and all its creatures. The process I offer in this book may be of some help.

Endnotes

1. Rainer Maria Rilke, *Letters To A Young Poet,* trans. by M. D. Herter Norton (New York: W. W. Norton and Company, Inc., 1954), p. 35.

2. I realize the word "feminist" carries a variety of meanings for readers. Because in its root form it refers to women, it can be considered to exclude men. However, current, but not universal usage, includes both women and men. In the context of this book, a feminist is a person, woman or man, who believes in the essential equality between women and men and seeks to create social attitudes, policies and structures that reveal and sustain that equality.

3. Barbara Bergmann, *The Economic Emergence Of Women* (New York: Basic Books, Inc., 1986), pp. 20-21.

4. Carol S. Robb, "A Framework for Feminist Ethics," in *Women's Consciousness, Women's Conscience* (Minneapolis: Winston Press, 1985), p. 211.

1

Living the Questions

Everything that has ever
helped me has come through what already
lay stored in me. Old things, diffuse, unnamed, lie strong
across my heart.

This is from where
my strength comes, even when I miss my strength
even when it turns on me
like a violent master.

—Adrienne Rich[1]

Each of us has a story of feminist conversion to tell. Mine begins back in 1969 in the office of a university professor. I was a graduate student of English at Florida State University. I also had the rather dubious distinction of being the only nun in the English Department. I was just finishing a review of my dissertation topic when the professor—a man—leaned back in his chair and declared in his typically avuncular manner, "You are the only woman in the English Department I don't mind working with." For a few precious moments, in my naivete, I thought maybe it was because I was the smartest. But my awareness of many talented women colleagues quickly erased that error while the professor continued, "You won't waste your education by getting married and having children." I left his office angry, confused, and convinced that I had just encountered something that was extremely unfair and fundamentally wrong.

Although it was 1969 and I had participated in the civil rights and anti-war movements, the "women's movement" was only a flicker on my horizon. Most of what I knew about it I had learned through the media,

1

and, needless to say, that source was hardly able or inclined at that time to give a fair hearing to the courageous women who were the first to raise their voices against the injustice and abuse women endure in our society. At that time the "women's movement" was extraneous to my concerns.

That crucial conversation changed my perspective. I began paying more attention to the lives and experiences of my women colleagues. I also learned that because I was a nun I walked around in a rather protective bubble. I was not subject to the kind of sexual harassment that so many of the women endured. Nor was I carrying multiple responsibilities in addition to my academic work. Many of the women students were married and had children, and thus were carrying the triple role of student, mother and spouse. While I worked as a student-teacher to finance my degree, I did not feel the same economic stresses that many of the other women felt. I knew that any financial crisis would be covered by my community. Other women, lacking the financial backup I had, carried part or full-time jobs in addition to being students. Several were single heads of households, widowed or divorced, and had returned to school to become better equipped to support their families. I began to know and to participate in the struggles of these women to fulfill their dreams despite the burdens and the institutional sexism they experienced.

However, I did not fully identify with the struggles of women until I was elected into leadership in my religious community.[2] This responsibility brought me into consistent contact with the Catholic hierarchy and clergy. It was also the period of time when religious communities were in the process of renewal, of rediscovering the charism of their founders and of testing how best to live that charism in the contemporary world. In discussions with pastors and bishops concerning just salaries for sisters, choice of clothing, residence, work, or the desire of the women to use their skills and talents in a variety of ways in the parishes and the larger community, I discovered among the clergy and hierarchy the unexamined presumption that they had the right to make these decisions for the individual women and the communities. Significant amounts of time were spent protecting both the individual sister's right and the community's right to define their life in ministry. The struggle against patriarchy and institutional sexism had become my personal struggle.

Initially my energies were focused on specific causes. The ERA (Equal Rights Amendment) was the first. I was living in a state which had not ratified the ERA. Within the church my agenda focused on inclusive language, ordination and the rather generic idea of justice for women, which included a variety of issues: altar girls, decision-making, preaching, etc.

In 1975, the International Women's Year challenged me to enlarge my view to include the causes of women outside the U.S. It was not until I joined the staff at the Center of Concern, Washington, DC, in 1979, however, that I had the opportunity to engage seriously in the questions that women from other countries were raising.

Meanwhile, the women's movement was beginning to organize within the Catholic church. Its first public expression was the Women's Ordination Conference in Detroit, 1975. The first Episcopalian women had been ordained in 1974 and the Detroit meeting was the opening of the question of women's ordination in the Roman church. In 1977, the Vatican responded to these events with "The Vatican Declaration on the Question of the Admission of Women to the Ministerial Priesthood." The answer was and continues to be "no." The long and painful dialogue between Catholic women and their church had begun.

Each Catholic feminist has her/his own story to tell in that dialogue. There are certain moments when the dialogue took place in the public forum: the Second Women's Ordination Conference in Baltimore in 1978; the encounter between Theresa Kane, RSM, and Pope John Paul II on the occasion of his first visit to the U.S. in 1979; Women Moving Church, a conference sponsored by the Center of Concern in 1981; the Vatican's forcing Agnes Mary Mansour to choose between her membership in the Sisters of Mercy and her ministry as director of the Michigan State Department of Human Services in a dispute over her responsibilities regarding the use of public funds for abortions among poor women in 1983; the emergence of Womenchurch at the Chicago meeting, "From Generation to Generation Womenchurch Speaks," in 1983 and a second national meeting, "Claiming Our Power," in Cincinnati in 1987; the conflict between the Vatican and the signers of the *New York Times* ad calling for dialogue on abortion in 1984; and the bishops' process for the writing of the pastoral on women's concerns in 1987.[3]

But such a listing of events does not speak to the struggle that individual women have carried on daily in parishes, in theological schools, on pastoral teams in hospitals, at student centers in colleges and universities, in board rooms and staff rooms, wherever Catholic feminists meet the institution and seek equality for women. My personal story includes both the public and personal events. I have known the joy of participating in women's strength and vitality as womenchurch. I have also known pain, anxiety, confusion, anger and frustration at the patriarchy and misogyny of churchmen. But that experience has been balanced by the deep friendship, support and encouragement I have known from many men—priests, bishops, and laymen—in my struggle for justice for women. They have taught me their own need of liberation and how our struggles are intimately linked. All of these experiences have fused into a quiet determination to continue to pursue the work of justice for women.

One important public church event that was not ostensibly focused on women's concerns had great influence in shaping my search. In 1975, I worked on the staff for the National Conference of Catholic Bishops' (NCCB) bicentennial program. The theme of the program was "Liberty and Justice for All." It sought to raise the issues of economic, racial and political justice within the larger national celebration of the U.S. bicentennial. It was also a call to the People of God to become involved in the church's mission of justice and peace. The final event of the two-year process was the meeting in Detroit, "A Call to Action," in 1976.

"A Call to Action" was a watershed moment in the U.S. Catholic church. For the first time, women and men, sisters, priests, bishops, archbishops and cardinals gathered to discuss issues of importance to the life of the church and the society. The issue of justice in the church was central in all its deliberations, and the call for justice for women in the church emerged from numerous caucus groups. The final report contained many controversial recommendations, including the ordination of women and married clergy, inclusive language, equality for women in all church structures, and altar girls. It also revealed a growing number of people within the church who questioned the church's patriarchy and hierarchy.

Within the existing structures of the church, "A Call to Action" could only be consultatory to the NCCB. Most of its recommendations have not been acted upon, but it is commonly held by many church professionals that the event opened the way for the consultation processes the bishops have used in writing the peace pastoral, the pastoral on the U.S. economy, and the pastoral on women's concerns. It also created renewed interest in Catholic social teaching and in the church's mission of justice and peace within the Catholic community in the U.S. The event deepened and expanded my long-time commitment to focus my energies on the church's mission for justice.

For me, these experiences revealed both the potential power of the church to be a force for justice in the world as well as its entrenched patriarchy. My search for a perspective that would bring together the strengths of my feminist commitment and my faith commitment had begun. In struggling to bring these two realities together, I came to realize that my commitment to the liberation of women was not only about justice for women, it was also about the integrity of the gospel and the authenticity and effectiveness of the church's mission of justice and peace in our age.

When I joined the staff of the Center of Concern in 1979, my work for justice for and with women became multi-faceted: women in the church, women in poverty, feminist theory, work and family issues, and women in development. My engagement with women, particularly from the countries of the Southern hemisphere, revealed to me the complexity of the issues behind the specific agendas when we seek justice for all women. Two sets of issues immediately began to surface for me: economic and cultural.

The economic issues demanded recognition of the interrelatedness of local, national, and international economies and their impact on women. We cannot work to move women beyond poverty without ultimately asking fundamental questions about the shape of the world's economy: who's rich, who's poor and why? These questions need to be asked domestically, nationally, and internationally. They begin to reveal how women's lives are circumscribed not only by patriarchy and the sexual division of labor, but also by national development strategies and the international structures of capitalism.

This fact raised a disturbing challenge. I cannot ignore the fact that I reap untold benefits from the present structures of international capitalism. I found myself asking if I really wanted equality for myself and other middle-class women in a world marred by such inequalities among various peoples and nations. I also found myself growing increasingly uncomfortable in the professional "women in development" community. While this group of women work very hard to support and create income-generating projects for women in the so-called Third World countries, they had no critique of the structures of international capitalism and the role of the United States in those structures. I began to realize that my commitment to equality had to include not only equality between women and men, but also equality among all peoples and all nations. That commitment had to involve criticism of the structures that generate inequality, as well as work toward the transformation of these structures.

Cultural issues proved to be even more subtle. What, if anything, does the feminism of Western industrialized nations have to offer women from other parts of the world? Is feminism ethnocentric—shaped by Western industrial values—or universal?[4] When we talk so glibly about women's experience, which women's experience are we using as normative? Is U.S. feminism, despite its sincere desire to be in solidarity with all women, yet another form of cultural imperialism? How does the experience of women from profoundly different cultures enlarge both the meaning and the agenda of the women's movement in the U.S.? This challenge has also been raised by Afro-American, Latina, Native American, and Asian women within the U.S. context. My initial easy assumptions about how to achieve equality for women were shattered.

It also became clear to me that any analysis of most women's lives demands an understanding of the interaction women maintain between work and family responsibilities. For a variety of complex social, cultural, and economic reasons, women cannot be isolated from the context of their relationships and dealt with as autonomous individuals in the same way that society permits and even encourages men to be.

For example, in the movie *Kramer vs. Kramer,* the audience feels sorry for Mr. Kramer when his career is interrupted suddenly by having to respond to the needs of his son. This dual demand and its choices are the daily experience of mothers working outside the home—a reality society takes for granted. Any analysis of women's reality demands a recognition of women's multiple roles in society.

This realization began to raise new and tricky questions that would need to be considered in charting a strategic path toward women's equality. How do we understand women's unique contributions to human society without restricting their potential within traditional fixed and sexist categories? How do we define agenda and public policy issues that sustain women in their multiple roles while not limiting their access to the full range of human activity? The growing "feminization of poverty" is a consistent reminder that we have not yet effectively analyzed nor found solutions to women's unique problems, economically, socially or politically. Furthermore, the disproportionate number of minority women among the women in poverty also demands that we understand the racial equation that shapes women's lives: Both the inherent privilege white women unconsciously enjoy in our society and the particular experience of women who are not from the dominant white culture. Racism remains a central problem in our society. These questions are internal to the women's movement as well.

I believe the abortion question remains the Gordian knot of the contemporary women's movement. While many national women's organizations maintain the "the right to choose" as a priority item, many people, women and men alike, bring grave reservations, if not outright opposition, to this position. Within the pluralism of the U.S., there is no moral consensus on the question of abortion. Even many who accept the political necessity of the "right to choose" within a pluralistic society are quick to say that personally, they do not believe in abortion.

Unfortunately, the lines of the argument and of political action have been rigidly drawn around two battle cries: "pro-choice" and "pro-life."

Please excuse the military language, but indeed it is appropriate. As the battle rages between these two forces, serious reflection on the arguments of both sides has little opportunity to surface in the process of shaping a moral consensus.

All too often, the "pro-life" advocates refuse to admit the legitimacy of the real survival problems women experience. Often they oppose welfare and other forms of government support that would sustain a woman and her child beyond the initial act of birth. They fixate their sole concern on the unborn. There is also the pervading problem that many "pro-life" advocates are very selective on whose life is to be preserved. Many in the movement are also "pro-capital punishment," "pro-unlimited defense," "pro-anti-communism" to the point of advocating military intervention, an innocent-sounding term that means war and killing to many innocent people. They lack a consistent ethic of life which, when embraced, demands a consistent ethic of justice.[5]

The "pro-choice" position raises the moral dilemma of "Claims in Conflict."[6] Yes, women have the right to the integrity of their own bodies. Yes, women have the moral capacity and the responsibility to make decisions concerning their bodies. But, what about the rights of the unborn? The rights of the father? The rights of society? What are the responsibilities that accompany these rights? Does one set of rights deny all others? How do we adjudicate these conflicts of rights?

The highly-charged political focus on "pro-life" and "pro-choice" has clouded other questions we should be addressing. For example, what are the economic structures that discriminate against women, militating against their ability to support a child? What work structures frustrate and limit women's potential if they have family responsibilities? What cultural norms and expectations are shaping a woman's decision to have or not have a child? How do cultural and social norms create so much irresponsibility in some men toward the children they father? How has society failed women? How has society failed children? What role has the church played? And finally, how do we create the environment to dialogue about this profoundly important human issue?

I am not alone nor even particularly original in the questions, issues, problems, and roadblocks I have encountered in my work for justice for women. But in seeking solutions and in working to develop public policy to support women's struggle for justice, I began to find myself uncomfortable with some of the prevailing "women's agenda" that I encountered. At first I thought it was simply a matter of strategy; that is, I did not believe that a particular choice of strategy would effect the common goal we all desired. But then I began to suspect that the differences were more than strategic, that in fact they were also ideological. I found I did not agree that some of the arguments put forth to support an agenda or a position carried the potential not only for women's liberation but for human liberation.

For example, in a keynote address at the 1985 conference, *Women Mean Business,* Adele Scheele, an author and career analyst stated, "At this stage, most of us are trailblazers—the first woman executive in a company, the first female in an occupation. The issue is who is going to make it and who isn't. And the people who are going to make it are going to be like those already on top. It's nice to think of more caring female managers, but those who care will never get to the top."[7] The prevailing model of success and its oppressive nature is not questioned; the goal is to move women into that model at all costs.

This realization began my investigation into the philosophic roots of U.S. feminism. In the process I discovered several different philosophic/ideologic strands that feed modern feminism. The dominant strands include liberal feminism, radical feminism, socialist feminism, and cultural feminism. Moreover, these ideologies do not go unchallenged. Women outside the dominant white culture of the U.S.—Afro-American women, Native American, Latina, and Asian women—challenge the assumption that these strands speak to their experience as minority women in the U.S. Women in the global women's movement outside this country raise fundamental challenges to the narrow range of issues that the U.S. women's movement addresses. Anti-feminist women actively work against the movement. And many women, while they certainly disagree with patriarchy and its negative effect on them as women, do not identify with feminism as they have experienced it. They are the women who preface their critique of patriarchy with "I'm not a feminist, but. . . ." The pluralism among women begs the question on the meaning of the word "feminism" and of the direction of the movement.

While feminists from all the dominant ideological stands claim a common goal—justice for women—they do not necessarily agree on the causes of women's oppression, nor on what will constitute justice for women. Strategically, the agendas of the various strands often overlap, and it is evident how each has enriched the analysis of our understanding of women's reality in our economic, social, political, and ecclesial systems. They have also mutually enriched each other's perspective. So, in fact, we do not have one feminist analysis or a single historic tradition, but a rich amalgam that informs our contemporary feminist understanding. Nevertheless, among these various strands there are also some major philosophic and strategic differences. For me the question emerged, what do I mean when I define myself as a feminist? Where do I fit in this picture?

This question directed my personal research and analysis as I unraveled the multi-strands of modern feminism, identifying its philosophic roots and analyzing the contribution each brings to our understanding of women's oppression. In the process I have discovered both the richness and the limitations of each approach and the questions I continue to have. When I have shared this research with others, they too have found it helpful in identifying themselves within the rich current of contemporary feminism. Their enthusiasm and encouragement prompted me to write this book.

The inevitable question that people ask is, "Well, which kind of a feminist are you?" My answer, "All and none." I have learned a great deal from each of the ideological strands of feminism; they each have contributed to the evolution of the women's liberation. But I cannot embrace any of them as a fully adequate perspective either on the human person or on human society. This realization brings me to the current phase of my story, though it certainly does not signal the end of my search.

As is obvious from my story, my Roman Catholic faith and my membership in the church are important dynamics in my search. My faith is a fundamental dimension of my identity. I am who I am today because I was born into an Irish Catholic family; attended Catholic grade school, high school, and college; entered a community of sisters, the Adrian

Dominicans, and have been publicly identified with the church throughout my adult life.

Like most things in life, this reality is a mixed blessing. The institutional church, with its historic and entrenched patriarchy remains a central problem for me as a feminist. So I live in the ambiguity of being a Catholic feminist/feminist Catholic. Yet, while struggling with the church to move it beyond patriarchy, I also find myself enriched by the faith tradition. It has been the richness of that faith tradition, particularly in its articulation of Catholic social thought and in its social mission, that has enlarged my reflection around the questions of women's liberation. The pastoral documents of the Second Vatican Council with their imaging of the church as the "People of God" and their call to "read the signs of the times" have situated the women's movement within the larger context of God's creative action in the world. The insights of liberation theology have enabled me to understand and affirm my struggle for the liberation of women. So for me, my feminism and my Catholicism have become mutually formative in my quest for a transformed church and world.

The very questions that continue to appear in my story clearly say that my search for an adequate framework to understand the struggle of women's liberation for a more whole and holy church and society is not over. This book, analyzing the various streams of contemporary feminism, is part of that on-going search. The unique perspective it brings to the already substantial and growing body of literature on feminist theory is the dialogue with Catholic social teaching.

This perspective will be considered an intrusion by some feminists who would assert that the admission of religious frameworks, although of some historical relevance, are implausible and outside contemporary feminist theory.[8] Not only do I believe that position is theoretically flawed, as I will try to demonstrate in the chapters that follow, I also believe it ignores the profound contribution of the many women who bring their particular religious perspective to their understanding and struggle for women's liberation. That position does not recognize the activity of God in the process of human liberation.

Finally, I identify this book as part of my on-going search because I do not believe at the present time that we have clarity on the multiple issues raised by the women's movement. I also realize that liberation is a process we are all called to be involved in. It is not a grand ideological, philosophical or theological scheme to be imposed upon us. But I do believe that we all work out of certain recognized or unrecognized ideological frameworks. Understanding these frameworks allows greater freedom to identify and clarify our commitment to a process of liberation that is consonant with our deepest beliefs in what it means to be part of the "People of God."

Process Questions

1. What is your feminist conversion story?

2. What events were particularly transforming?

3. What did you learn from them?

In this chapter, I have touched upon some of the important elements of my personal story. Personal stories are part of larger historical moments. The contemporary women's movement spans the 19th and 20th centuries. The "second wave" of that movement is twenty-five years old. Chapter Two will give a brief overview of that history in its relationship to other key historical events. Out of knowledge of that past, we can gain a perspective to chart the future. So I end this story where I began:

> *Everything that has ever*
> *helped me has come through what already*
> *lay stored in me. Old things, diffuse, unnamed, lie strong*
> *across my heart.*

> *This is from where*
> *my strength comes, even when I miss my strength*
> *even when it turns on me*
> *like a violent master.*
> —Adrienne Rich

Endnotes

1. "Sources," in *Your Native Land, Your Life* (New York: W.W. Norton and Company, 1986), p. 4.

2. The use of the term "religious" to describe one kind of life-style in the church is problematic for me. Unwittingly such usage denies the religious dimensions of all life-styles. I prefer the term "canonical community," but because that term is not as readily understood, I will use the more common term religious.

3. For a more extended treatment of these events, I refer you to *New Catholic Women: A Contemporary Challenge To Traditional Religious Authority* by Mary Jo Weaver (San Francisco: Harper and Row Publishers, 1985); and "Women, Church and Patriarchy" by Maria Riley, OP in *America*, Vol. 150, No. 17 (May 4, 1984). Reprints of this article are available from the Center of Concern.

4. Irene Tinker raised this question during a keynote address in 1982, at a conference on "Concepts and Strategies: Women's Studies in Different Cultures." An adaptation of that talk was printed as an occasional paper for Equity Policy Center, Washington, DC.

5. The term "consistent ethic of life" was first used by Joseph Cardinal Bernardin as a moral perspective that would include not only the defense of all forms of life but also the advocacy of social policy that supports people's rights to a dignified form of human life, including such human necessities as food, housing, clothes, medical care, education, work, and leisure.

6. This phrase is taken from the title of a book in a series from the Woodstock Theological Center: *Claims in Conflict: Retrieving and Renewing the Catholic Human Rights Tradition* by David Hollenbach, S.J. (New York: Paulist Press, 1979).

7. As quoted in "Sisterhood Under Seige" by Richard Moore and Elizabeth Marsis in *The Progressive* (January, 1985), p. 30.

8. Alison M. Jaggar, *Feminist Politics and Human Nature* (Totowa, New Jersey: Rowman and Allanheld, 1983), p. 10.

2

We Hold These Truths

We hold these truths to be self-evident
that all men [sic] are created equal.

With these words the great American experiment in freedom was launched. This experiment led first to the Revolutionary War and eventually to the Civil War. It also initiated a longer and still unresolved struggle in the United States: The struggle for equality between the sexes. Abigail Adams issued the first gentle but prophetic warning in a letter to her husband, March, 1776:

> I long to hear that you have declared an independancy—and by the way in the new Code of Laws which I suppose it will be necessary for you to make I desire you would Remember the Ladies, and be more generous and favourable to them than your ancestors. Do not put such unlimited power into the hands of the Husbands. Remember all Men would be tyrants if they could. If perticuliar care and attention is not paid to the Laidies we are determined to foment a Rebelion, and will not hold ourselves bound by any Laws in which we have no voice, or Representation.[1]

To which her husband, John, responded:

> As to your extraordinary Code of Laws, I cannot but laugh. We have been told that our Struggle has loosened the bands of Government every where. That Children and Apprentices were disobedient—that schools and Colleges were grown turbulent—that Indians slighted their Guardians and Negroes grew insolent to their Masters. But your letter was the first intimation that another Tribe more numerous and powerfull than all the rest were grown discontented.[2]

To this day, that "tribe" remains discontent after more than a century of women's struggle to achieve equal rights and opportunities within the

14

American dream. The contemporary expression of that struggle, the feminist movement, has built on the courage and tenacity of the women who came before us.

Historical Roots

The nineteenth-century women's rights movement reflected the Enlightenment perspective of the common and universal nature of all persons. This perspective shaped both the Declaration of Independence and the Constitution of the new republic. But in reality, its rhetoric of universality applied only to land-owning white males.

Mary Wollstonecraft was the first woman to include women in that perspective. Her classic *On the Vindication of the Rights of Women,* published in London in 1792, was the first liberal feminist publication. Arguing that women's historical deficiencies were the product of their socialization, Wollstonecraft advocated equal educational opportunities to free women from the ignorance, servitude, and dependency to which social custom condemned them.

Written with impassioned rhetoric, *On the Vindication of the Rights of Women* gained popularity on both sides of the Atlantic. Four American and six British editions were printed during the nineteenth century. Evidence of Wollstonecraft's influence is apparent in such early American feminists as Sarah Grimke, who based her gender analysis on the Enlightenment assumption that women and men are not only moral and intellectual equals, but ontologically the same.[3]

Deeply shaped by the doctrine of the equality of all persons, the nineteenth-century women's rights movement discovered itself within the abolition movement. Although women were active in anti-slavery work, suffering the verbal abuse and physical violence often vented against abolitionists, they were forbidden to take public roles. Leadership, with its public visibility and power, was reserved to men. At the World Anti-Slavery Convention in London, 1840, the women delegates were not allowed to speak nor to sit on the main floor of the convention hall. Elizabeth Cady Stanton and Lucretia Mott, delegates to that meeting, met in the balcony. Eight years later, these two women spearheaded the first Women's Rights Convention in 1848 at Seneca Falls, New York.

At that historic meeting, the delegates adopted the Seneca Falls Declaration, the single most important women's rights document of nineteenth-century America. Pointedly written in the language of the Declaration of Independence, the Seneca Falls Declaration takes up Abigail Adams' challenge by stating: "We hold these truths to be self-evident; that all men and women are created equal; that they are endowed by their Creator with certain inalienable rights, that among these are life, liberty and the pursuit of happiness. . . ."[4] The Declaration continues with a list of grievances which outline how men have deprived women of their inalienable rights. The listing includes denial of the right to vote, no representation in government, lack of civil and property rights, lack of rights within the marital contract, taxation without representation, and lack of equal economic, social, and professional opportunity. The agenda for women's equality was set.

The initial union of the anti-slavery movement and the women's rights movement called for universal suffrage for all women and men, black and white. But post-Civil War white male politics split that union, setting suffrage for black men over against suffrage for women. White women responded with a fury against being considered less than former slaves and concentrated all their energy on gaining the vote for themselves. Black women became invisible in the dispute. This wound of racism within the women's movement has never been totally healed.

The nineteenth-century cult of "ideal womanhood"[5] was the primary cultural argument against granting suffrage to women. The churches were a major voice supporting this ideology of femininity, arguing against women's right to vote. In an interview with the *New York Globe* (June 22, 1911), Cardinal Gibbons declared:

> Women's suffrage, . . . I am surprised that one should ask the question. I have but one answer to such a question, and that is that I am unalterably opposed to women's suffrage, always have been and always will be. . . . Why should a woman lower herself to sordid politics? Why should a woman leave her home and go into the streets to play the game of politics? Why should she long to come into contact with men at the polling places? Why should she long to rub elbows with men who are her inferiors intellectually and morally? Why should a woman long to go into streets and leave behind her happy home, her children, a husband and everything that goes to make up an ideal domestic life? . . . When

a woman enters the political arena, she goes outside the sphere for which she was intended. She gains nothing by that journey. On the other hand, she loses the exclusiveness, respect and dignity to which she is entitled in her home.

Who wants to see a woman standing around the polling places, speaking to a crowd on the street corner: pleading with those in attendance at a political meeting? Certainly such a sight would not be relished by her husband or by her children. Must the child, returning from school, go to the polls to find his [sic] mother? Must the husband returning from work, go to the polls to find his wife, soliciting votes from this man and that? . . . Woman is queen, but her kingdom is the domestic kingdom.[6]

Such statements by clergymen, subtly linking women's struggle for equality to sexual promiscuity and defining the "ideal" woman's role solely within the context of family, gave a moral credibility to those who opposed women's suffrage. This kind of statement, reflecting centuries of the churches' negative and limiting theological perspectives on women, provides the evidence for many women's bitter attacks against religion as a major cause and support of women's historical subordination. This criticism is historically justified.

However, the efforts of the women's rights movement survived the attacks and agendas of both the white male political machine and white patriarchal religions. The 19th amendment to the Constitution, granting women the right to vote, was finally passed in 1920. With this success, the white middle-class membership of the women's movement declared that the fight for women's equality had been won.

But a small militant wing of the movement, the National Women's Party, declared that suffrage had achieved little and women were "still subordinated to men before the law, in the professions, in the churches, in industry, and in the home." Under the leadership of Alice Paul, the National Women's Party succeeded in getting the Equal Rights Amendment (ERA) introduced into Congress in 1923. In each succeeding year it was re-introduced into Congress until 1972, when the Amendment was finally passed and sent out to the states for ratification.

The passage of the 19th Amendment was not the only achievement of the nineteenth-century women's rights movement. Their work to establish equality for women included changes in laws to insure women's property rights, universal general education for girls and women, protective labor laws for women and children (now under attack by contemporary feminists), and some small breakthroughs into the professions.

The tragic events that engulfed the United States during the 1930s and 1940s, the Great Depression and the outbreak of World War II, eclipsed the questions of women's equality. Questions of survival engaged women and men first in New Deal programs for economic recovery, and then in war efforts at home and abroad.

While not specifically advocating women's rights, a growing number of women were exercising political power and influence, as well as some leadership roles, in both the Democratic party and in labor. For example, Frances Perkins held the Cabinet post of Secretary of Labor from 1933-1945, and the Women's Bureau in the Department of Labor, established in 1920, continued to increase its prominence.[8] This cadre of women was known as "feminists in the 'woodwork' of national politics."[9] Likewise, the role of "Rosie the Riveter," who personified that corps of women who went to work in factories during World War II, has become legendary. Equally legendary is the social pressure exerted on these women to return to the home after World War II.

Meanwhile, the women's organizations founded during the late nineteenth and early twentieth centuries were building a wide constituency and leadership base for the future. The roster of these organizations carries a persistent record of women's dedication to equality: The American Association of University Women (AAUW) dates back to 1882; the Young Women's Christian Association (YWCA) was churchwomen's response to the plight of the young workingwoman in the sweatshops of industrial cities; the General Federation of Women's Clubs, 1890, was founded to support professional women; the National Association of Colored Women's Clubs, 1896, was formed to circumvent the racism in the General Federation of Women's Clubs and to advance the liberation of black people; the Women's International League for Peace and Freedom, 1915, was a women's peace initiative to respond to World War I; the League of Women Voters, 1920, formed to educate the new female electorate; and the National Federation of Business and Professional Women's Clubs, 1919, evolved from the U.S. War Department's Women's War Council. All these organizations "gained in strength and status throughout the twenties and thirties when millions of American women came together in weekly or monthly meetings to discuss civic, business, cultural and personal problems and solutions."[10] Quietly, these women were preparing the way for the second wave of the women's movement that was to break upon the American scene during the 1960s.

The Second Wave—The 60s

Historians set the year of Betty Friedan's *The Feminine Mystique*, 1963, as the identifiable moment for the beginning of the second wave of the women's movement in the United States.* However, *The Feminine Mystique* had a ready audience prepared by a variety of events. Feminism as we know it today has its roots in the complex social and political history of the 1960s. Out of that history, three distinct evolutionary strands of the women's movement have shaped contemporary feminism: bureaucratic, organizational and collectivist.[11] The bureaucratic strand includes those historical agencies and events that are linked to government initiatives, such as the Women's Bureau of the U. S. Department of Labor. The organizational strand follows the evolution of women's organizations with well-defined structures, such as the League of Women Voters and the National Organization for Women (NOW). The collectivist strand charts the less structurally defined but very active grassroots women's groups that developed for consciousness-raising or for a special project, such as the founding of a shelter for battered women. Each strand carries its own historical and ideological perspectives, but all are woven into the fabric of contemporary feminism.

Bureaucratic History

Responding to the hundreds of women who had supported his campaign for the presidency, John F. Kennedy established a Presidential Commission on the Status of Women in December, 1961. Eleanor Roosevelt and Esther Peterson were appointed co-chairs. The Commission gave visibility to women and provided the vehicle for the first official report on the status of women in the United States, *American Women,* published in October, 1963. In response to the recommendations of the report, Kennedy set up the Interdepartmental Committee on the Status of Women, and the

*See Appendix A for a historical summary of the Women's Movement: 1963-1989.

Citizens' Advisory Council on the Status of Women. These two groups became important bodies with official status pressuring the government to live up to its public nondiscriminatory rhetoric. In addition, by 1963, following the lead of the federal government, many states had set up Commissions on the Status of Women.[12]

However, it was a typical political ploy of a Southern Congressman, Howard Smith, that became the catalyst for catapulting women into political activity. It was 1964, the year of the Civil Rights Bill. Congressman Smith wanted to defeat the pending civil rights legislation. Given the mood of the country, he knew he could not attack the legislation outright. So he devised the ploy of including women in Title VII, the equal employment section of the bill. With this addition, perhaps the bill could be laughed out of Congress. However, the ploy failed, due to the lobbying efforts of women and the pro-civil rights mood of the country. When the law went into effect in July, 1965, it became illegal to discriminate against women in hiring and promotions.[13]

But the struggle had just begun. When the Equal Employment Opportunity Commission (EEOC) was set up to enforce Title VII, neither the Executive Director nor the Commissioners took the gender clause seriously. Most of the Commissioners considered the clause a joke, and either ignored it or trivialized its intent.

But a network of women both inside and outside the government was already in place and watching. At the 1965 meeting of the National Conference of State Commissions, sponsored by the Citizens' Advisory Council and the Interdepartmental Committee on the Status of Women, the idea for an independent women's organization to lobby for women's rights was born. With Betty Friedan, author of *The Feminine Mystique,* as the first president, and 300 charter members, NOW, the National Organization for Women, was launched October 29, 1966. Its stated purpose was, "To take action to bring women into full participation in the mainstream of American society now, exercising all the privileges and responsibilities thereof in truly equal partnership with men."[14] The era of feminist organizations had begun.

Organizational History

As the founding of NOW illustrates, a clear symbiotic relationship existed—and continues to exist—between the bureaucratic and the organizational strands of the women's movement. The women involved knew each other, shared a common agenda, exchanged information and supported each other in their respective spheres. It was not unusual for the same women to function in both spheres.

The founding of NOW was a harbinger of the amazing eruption of feminist organizations that characterized the movement for the next decade. In 1970 a sixteen-page tabloid directory, called *The Mushroom Effect*, listed several hundred feminist organizations. By 1973, *Women Today*, an independent national newsletter, published a directory of several thousand groups.[15]

Even a selective listing will illustrate the energy so many women were bringing to the effort: WEAL (Women's Equity Action League) was founded in 1968; FEW (Federally Employed Women) in 1968; Women's Action Alliance, 1971; National Women's Political Caucus, 1971; Women's Lobby, Inc., 1972; National Black Feminist Organization, 1973. Many of the organizations concentrated on influencing government policy and expanding the role of women in government.

The momentum was increased further by the activities of many of the traditional women's organizations, such as the League of Women Voters, the American Association of University Women and the National Council of Negro Women, which escalated their feminist agenda. The Equal Rights Amendment (ERA) became a central focus for much of their work.

Women in the labor unions took leadership in promoting women's offices and newsletters within their respective unions, traditional bastions of anti-feminist positions. By 1974 the labor union women were organized enough to form the Coalition of Labor Union Women (CLUW). Its objectives were not only to fight sexism within the labor unions, but also to work for legislation on behalf of women. They endorsed the ERA, contrary to the traditional AFL/CIO position.[16]

Both the bureaucratic and organizational strands of the movement worked in concert to effect changes within the existing political, economic, and social structures. While they may have differed in perspectives or priorities, basically they carried on 19th century equal rights feminism.

The challenge for a much more radical transformation of the status quo came from a very different set of historical events within the U.S. society, and found expression in the collectivist strand of the feminist movement. This strand moved the women's movement beyond equal rights feminism to women's liberation.

Collectivist History

The collectivist strand of feminism in the United States has its roots in the civil rights movement and the student-led new left movement of the 1960s. Like their foremothers in the nineteenth century women's rights movement, the young women who ignited the twentieth century women's liberation movement in the late 60s cut their political teeth in the civil rights and the anti-war movements. In working for the freedom of others, they discovered the profound sexism that dominated their own lives.

The young white women who joined the civil rights movement of the early 60s were, for the most part, the daughters of women who lived the cult of female domesticity that flourished during the 50s. When Betty Friedan wrote *The Feminine Mystique* in 1963, identifying the "problem that has no name," she tapped into a deep reservoir of white middle-American women's discontent. Educated and talented women everywhere, particularly in the suburbs, were finding their lives too narrow, boring, and isolated, as they tried to live up to the ideal housewife and mother image of the era. With the publication of *The Feminine Mystique,* individual women discovered they were not alone in their discontent. Furthermore, they were also witnessing the changing social and political scene inaugurated by the election of John F. Kennedy and the growing civil rights movement. They began to perceive a new world opening up.

Meanwhile, their daughters were stepping into new worlds that offered them a renewed sense of moral purpose and the opportunity to move beyond the cultural isolation of their mothers' suburban lives. Many young white women from the North and from the South broke with their middle-class backgrounds and joined the black community in sit-ins, marches, demonstrations, bus boycotts, freedom rides, and voter registration campaigns.

During the terrible early years of the movement, confronted with the violence of white resistance and the fear of rejection and intimidation from their own families and communities, these young women discovered great courage in the moral and religious ethos of the black civil rights community. In the Student Non-violent Coordinating Committee (SNCC) and the Southern Student Organizing Committee (SSOC), a cluster of young white women found themselves part of the "beloved community." These deeply religious groups of black and white civil rights activists shared a vision of non-violence and equality between the races not only for the future but also as part of the nature of the movement itself.[17] To this vision the young white women brought energy, dedication, talent and self-effacing hard work.

However, the experience also brought these young women face-to-face with the tangled web of race and sex. The combination of high idealism, practical innocence, and the intensity of the commitment left them vulnerable to the reality that, as white women, they were potent symbols of racial domination and naive targets for sexual exploitation.[18] Early stress points began to appear.

By the mid 60s, two currents fed a growing rupture in the "beloved community" that had been idealized in the early years of SNCC: The increasing discontent among the women over the supportive roles they were expected to play, and the terrible tenacity of racism in the white majority culture. Black women in the movement were the first to complain about special treatment given the white women. White women complained about the work they were expected to do: office maintenance, housecleaning, cooking, and emotional and sexual support. Furthermore, the violence of the white community's response to their attempts at non-violent action slowly eroded the hope that blacks and whites could live together mutually and peacefully. This erosion fed the rise of the Black Power movement within the Civil Rights movement. The movement was enlarging its focus from an appeal to the moral imperative of justice to an assertion of black power.[19]

These two currents converged at a SNCC retreat in 1964, when three women, Mary King, Casey Hayden, and Mary Varela, wrote an anonymous position paper on "Women in the Movement," which outlined sexual discrimination in SNCC. One of the SNCC heroes, Stokely Carmichael, quipped, "The only position for women in SNCC is prone."[20] This response has become legendary as one of the catalysts for the growing consciousness of women and for the anger that was eventually to explode in the women's liberation movement.

This simmering discontent was not confined to the civil rights movement, it was also alive in the student-led new left movement. This explosion of political energy and protest that marked student life during the mid-60s ignited from the combustible materials of racism, poverty, cultural alienation, the escalation of the war in Vietnam, and the assassination of heroes—John F. Kennedy, Robert Kennedy and Martin Luther King. Located primarily on college and university campuses, the movement generated a plethora of protest organizations: Students for a Democratic Society (SDS), Northern Student Movement (NSM), Student Peace Union, Berkeley Free Speech Movement (FSM), National Mobilization Against the War in Vietnam, Draft Resisters, and many more local groups.

These political agendas found their context within the growing counterculture, where the flower children, in rebellion against the lives of their parents, sought freedom from middle-American values. Woodstock, the great love-in musical festival held in the Catskills of New York state in 1969, became the symbol of this counterculture. This loose amalgam of groups was known as the new left.

While embracing the vision of a non-racist society, the character of new left groups differed widely from the southern civil rights organizations which focused on specific goals, such as black voter registration and the desegregation of buses, restaurants, movie houses, hotels. The student groups in the North were theoretical and intellectual in style. While engaging in some protest action, their main enthusiasm was to develop an ideological critique of American Society. In this effort, men dominated and competed for media and movement notoriety;[21] women did the organizing and support work.

The new left, rejecting the "old left" with its traditional communist and socialist parties linked to the Soviet Union, nevertheless identified with the marxist tradition of analysis and revolutionary action. Using the categories of marxist analysis, they developed a critique of U.S. capitalism and its "global imperialism." The new left brought its "revolutionary action" of debates, teach-ins, sit-ins, and demonstrations to bear against racism and poverty, but most vehemently against the U.S. war in Vietnam.[22]

Liberation movements became the focus of the new left's passion and rhetoric: black liberation within a white racist society; Third World countries' liberation from neo-colonial powers; sexual liberation from puritanical bonds; workers' liberation from the alienation of capitalism. But women's liberation from the patriarchy and sexism within the movements was a non-issue. The women who raised the issue were accused of distracting from the "important" work of liberation by their "middle-class" concerns.

Relegated to traditional supportive roles, the women found themselves in a very conflictive environment. Recognizing that the movement afforded them an opportunity to be engaged in significant action to challenge their country to live up to its own ideals of freedom and democracy, the women also recognized the failure of the new left to live up to its own ideals of liberation, participatory democracy, openness, fairness and equality with regard to them as women. With evident sarcasm, Lydia Sargent has defined the conflict well:

> Women working in new left and civil rights organizations were faced more and more with two main problems: (1) the problem of day-to-day work (who cleans the office/who messes it up, who writes leaflets/who types them, who talks at meetings/who takes notes, who gains status through sexual relations/who gives status through sexual relations) and; (2) the problem of theory (who leads the revolution, who makes it, who is liberated by it, and who keeps the home fires burning during it).[23]

When they attempted to raise the issue at meetings they were confronted with storms of protest, condescension, and sexually offensive remarks. The depth of hostility and contempt that greeted the women was inexplicable, but it fueled their growing anger which finally exploded at the National Conference for New Politics in Chicago, August 1967, when the women's resolution and the women who presented it were first ignored and then belittled when they insisted on a hearing.[24]

A week later Jo Freeman and Shulamith Firestone, organizers of the women's caucus at the Conference, convened a meeting of women in Chicago—the contemporary women's liberation movement was born.[25] From this beginning two groups emerged in Chicago: The Women's Radical Action Project and the Westside Group. Similar events fueled the founding of women's groups in Seattle and San Francisco. Shulamith Firestone went on to New York and joined with Pam Allen to organize the Radical Women.[26]

The women who met were schooled in the tactics of organizing that characterized the new left. Through an informal network of friends, newsletters, and personal communications, the word spread and women's groups sprang up in Boston, Detroit, New Orleans, Toronto, and Gainesville, Florida.

In early 1968, Jo Freeman started a newsletter, *Voice Of The Women's Liberation Movement,* to connect the rapidly expanding movement. The mailing list grew from 200 for the first issue in March, 1968, to over 2,000 for the seventh and last mailing sixteen months later. It grew in size from 6 to 25 pages.

Meanwhile another group of radical women was forming within NOW. In 1968, Ti-Grace Atkinson, then president of the New York Chapter of NOW, accompanied by other radical women, walked out of the NOW annual meeting in protest of NOW's hierarchical structure. They returned to New York City and founded The Feminists.

Using consciousness-raising as both an analytical and an organizing tool, groups of women gathered, began to develop a feminist analysis of their oppression as women, staged public actions to express their agenda and outrage, and experienced great exhilaration in the founding of the new movement.

The women's liberation movement first broke into public consciousness when a group of women demonstrated at the Miss America Contest in 1968. Protesting the commercialization of women as sex objects, the feminists staged a "freedom trash can" into which they threw make-up, fake eyelashes, girdles and bras. Although no bras were burned, it was this event that created the image of the "bra-burning" feminists. The media had a field day making the movement appear ridiculous, but the national attention generated a massive influx of new members into all branches of the women's movement. It was as if women everywhere were waiting for the signal to begin again their public march to liberation.[28]

In contrast to the organizational strand, the collectivists' groups were younger, movement oriented, often forming and re-forming in intense small communities of women. They were suspicious of traditional institutions, egalitarian, and anarchist in spirit. Their political actions took the form of public protests. Because the groups did not depend upon any organizational structure they could spring up wherever women gathered. Networking, often through personal contacts, became their organizational form.

However, lines of stress began to emerge early among the various collectivist women. In August of 1968, a group of twenty-two women, primarily from six cities with women's liberation groups—Chicago, New York, Boston, Washington, DC, Baltimore and Gainesville, Florida—met in Sandy Springs, Maryland, to determine whether the newly emerging groups should remain part of the new left or launch an independent movement. Unable to resolve their differences, they agreed to hold an open national conference in Chicago the following November.

Despite the short notice, lack of organization, and limited communication, over 200 women convened in Chicago. The diversity among the groups became immediately apparent. They had gathered together, but their historical and ideological roots were different. The lines of debate emerged between the radical women and the socialist women, and the disagreements were organizational, ideological, and strategic.

The socialist women, with political roots in the new left, had a ready-made ideology that provided both analytical and strategic direction. They identified so-called "women's issues" within a wider political agenda. The radicals did not share a coherent political past nor did they have a coherent ideology at that time. For the radicals, the oppression of women was the primary agenda. Furthermore, the women who had walked out of the new left, enraged by its sexism, had no interest in reconnecting with the men even as a strong women's movement. Nor did they believe that Marxist ideology or the new left adequately addressed women's issues. The debate was often bitter and remained unresolved. From this division two distinct feminist ideologies were to emerge in the early seventies: socialist feminism and radical feminism.[29]

Several attempts were made to unify the strands of the burgeoning women's movement. In November, 1969, some 500 women from both organizations, such as NOW and Women Lawyers—Boston, and collectivists' groups, held the First Congress to Unite Women. Despite differences these groups managed to develop a 10 point platform, including child care centers, repeal of anti-abortion laws, the ERA, equality in education and employment, as well as the end of sex-role socialization. In 1970, a Second Congress was held.[30]

The Women's Strike for Equality March in August 1970 was the most massive cooperative project. Coordinated by NOW, the strike drew women from across the political spectrum in major cities and small towns throughout the United States. The sheer numbers of women who turned out all across the U.S. surprised everyone, including the organizers. The Strike was the first time the potential power of the movement became public.[31] It also alerted the opposition.

Consolidation and Diffusion—The 70s

The Women' Strike for Equality in 1970 was a turning point for the women's movement; the re-founding phase was over. Women began to join forces for their common cause beyond the differences in their style, history, ideology, and organizational models. The bureaucratic, organizational, and collectivist strands continued to evolve, each making its distinctive contribution, while mutually sharing and shaping the emerging movement and its agenda. During the 70s, these groups, so different in origin, ideology, and strategy, learned to appreciate the unique kind of work each brought to the building up of the movement.

Bureaucratic and organizational women worked together and followed traditional methods to extend women's rights and opportunities within existing political, economic, and social systems. They spearheaded the Equal Rights Amendment campaign; lobbied the EEOC for women's work rights, including a strongly worded set of guidelines against sexual harassment; skillfully moved Title IX, the equal opportunity in education provision into the Education Act of 1972; identified and moved equal pay initiatives on local, state, and congressional levels; protected women's reproductive freedom (Roe vs. Wade, the Supreme Court decision protecting women's privacy rights in reproductive choices was handed down in 1973); worked to get women elected into political office as well as appointed into governmental positions; and addressed women's economic issues including pensions, Social Security for homemakers, and insurance rates.

Women's policy institutes developed to help lawmakers identify ways to extend women's rights. The Congressional Women's Caucus was founded in 1977 as a bipartisan effort "to promote legislation that will remedy inequities in public policy, eliminate economic disparities that handicap many women, and update existing programs to reflect the changes in women's lifestyles needs."[32] In 1981, reflecting the growing political power of women, the caucus changed its name to the Congressional Caucus for Women's Issues.

Having formed CLUW (Coalition of Labor Union Women) in 1974, labor women actively recruited blue-collar women into the movement. New unionizing efforts began among women officeworkers with the development of the semi-autonomous 9-to-5 groups. These efforts also began to enlarge the agenda of the women's movement to include blue-collar and pink-collar workers' needs.

Women who were not part of the dominant white culture also began to organize in order that their voice and agenda be heard. The 70s saw the emergence of the North American Indian Women's Association, Commission Feminil Mexicana, the National Conference of Puerto Rican Women, The National Black Feminist Organization, Mexican American Women National Association, Pan Asian American Women, the Organization of Chinese American Women and the Women of All Red Nations (WARN).[33] Alice Walker, a prominent black writer, named the womanist movement. A womanist is "a black feminist or feminist of color. From the black folk expression of mothers to female children, 'You acting womanish,' i.e., like a woman. Usually referring to outrageous, audacious, courageous or WILLFUL behavior. . . . Responsible. In charge. SERIOUS."[34] These efforts at self-definition challenge the white women's movement to recognize the diversity in and to be in solidarity with the larger women's movement.

Organizations too numerous to identify sprang up to protect women's legal and professional rights and opportunities. Women formed caucuses within existing organizations, while an unprecedented number of young women entered the professions—legal, medical, and financial—formerly the preserve of men.

Simultaneously, women from the collectivist strand developed nontraditional ways to work toward women's liberation. More interested in challenging systems than in working through them, they opened women's centers on college and university campuses; developed women's studies programs; opened rape crisis lines and centers for battered and abused women and children; set up women's health collectives; organized neighborhood women in self-help programs; created alternative economic enterprises; developed the women's cultural movement; and brought women's perspective and voice to the peace and ecology movements.

All such listings of women's activities fail to capture the explosion of energy. A recent publication, *Decade of Achievement: 1977—1987*, opens with a series of statistics to illustrate the growth of the movement:

• In 1970, no one even knew what a "battered women's shelter" was. Now there are at least 1200 such centers or shelters in the U.S.

• In 1969, there was one Women's Studies program. . . . Today, there are at least 503 Women's Studies programs in the U.S., serving approximately 250,000 students each year.

• Displaced homemakers were first recognized in the early 70s. Now there are over 1000 Displaced Homemaker groups, programs or services in the U.S.

• In 1970, no one had ever heard of a "women's center." A recent compilation by the National Association of Women's Centers has discovered that there are at least 4000 Women's Centers now in the U.S.

• The first women's newspaper sprang up in 1968-9. There are now at least 400 feminist newspapers, 110 women's presses and publishers, and 10 women's news services in the U.S. or linking American feminists with counterparts in other parts of the world.

• The percentage of women in municipal elective office has tripled since 1975 (4% women to 14% women). Women hold the position of mayor in 11 of America's 100 largest cities. In state legislatures, in 1987, women held 15.6% of elected positions, up from 4% in 1969.

• Women have been going into business three times faster than men. There are now 3.3 million women business owners, up 33% since 1976.

• In 1976, *Ladyslipper Catalogue* was founded in Durham, NC, by an all-volunteer group who wanted to promote woman-produced (not just woman-performed) music. The first catalogue had 16 pages, and less than 200 entries. Today, *Ladyslipper* is a wholesale supplier with six major outlets nationwide, an annual volume of 50,000 tapes or records, and their catalogue runs to 80 pages with over 1200 entries, including music by feminist men and non-sexist children's music.[35]

Tracing the extraordinary growth of the movement in the 70s is virtually impossible, but several key events do provide a focus: the struggle for the Equal Rights Amendment (ERA); the International Women's Decade (IWD), 1975-1985; and the First Women's National Conference in Houston, 1977.

The ERA

Forty-nine years after it was first introduced into Congress, the House of Representatives and the Senate approved the Equal Rights Amendment (ERA) in 1972. The language of the amendment is straightforward:

1. Equality of rights under the law shall not be denied or abridged by the United States or by any State on account of sex.

2. The Congress shall have power to enforce by appropriate legislation the provisions of this article.

3. The Amendment shall take effect two years after the date of ratification.

Ratification of the ERA galvanized women from all strands of the movement. It became the rallying cry and the central symbol of women's new consciousness. As such it was able to unite women across the political spectrum, enabling bureaucratic, organizational, and collectivist women to join forces on a common agenda. Representative Martha Griffiths of Michigan was only able to move the amendment through Congress because women everywhere had been mobilized to write their Congresspersons demanding the endorsement. This mobilization was spearheaded by the Ad Hoc Committee for the ERA. The committee used existing national women's organizations', Unions' and networks' mailing lists to initiate a national lobbying campaign.[36]

Congressional approval was followed by relatively rapid ratification by thirty-four of the required thirty-eight states. However, the opposition forces grew in strength. In 1973, Phyllis Schlafly, a conservative, founded the "Stop ERA" campaign, giving religious and political conservatives a rallying point. The issues the conservatives raised—single-sex bathrooms, women in combat, homosexual marriages, breakdown of the family, men failing to support their families, and abortion—tapped deeply into traditional and religious feelings and anxieties about the roles of women and men. Women's rights advocates expanded and accelerated their efforts, but they underestimated the skill, dedication, and passion of their opponents. The ERA failed to capture the required number of state ratifications and died in 1982. It was re-introduced into Congress on January 3, 1983, but lies temporarily dormant as women have addressed their energies to other issues.[37]

The International Women's Decade (IWD)

Early in the 1970s, the United Nations, at the suggestion of the UN Commission on the Status of Women, named 1975 the International Women's Year (IWY). In 1972 the U.S. State Department set up an Interagency Group to plan the U.S. Government's participation in the IWY. Early in 1975, President Gerald Ford established the National Commission for the International Women's Year with 35 members representing a wide constituency of women in the U.S.

The National Commission set into motion a cooperative venture which included over 200 traditional, labor union, and feminist organizations. The State Department IWY Secretariat became staff to the National Commission. A flurry of activity followed, developing both a national women's agenda and an international women's focus.[38]

This activity culminated at the IWY Meeting in Mexico City during the summer of 1975. Over 7000 women from all parts of the world gathered in Mexico City to participate in the event. There were two meetings: the official government-to-government meeting under the aegis of the United Nations and The Tribune, the non-governmental parallel forum open to all women. That meeting was touted as the "greatest consciousness-raising event in history."

It proved to be both exhilarating and shattering for many U.S. women participants. For many it was the first time they were involved in global politics. They were unprepared for the crass manipulation of the agenda at the official meeting by traditional governmental politics. Furthermore, meeting women from around the world at The Tribune broke many U.S. women out of the national ghetto they had known all their lives. Discovering common experiences of women amid enormous cultural, political, and economic diversity created many bonds. But the meeting also forced many U.S. women to look at the dominant political and economic role of the U.S. around the world. The anger of many women toward the U.S. was shocking and confusing.

At Mexico City, women's global consciousness was born. With the U.N. declaring 1975-1985 the International Women's Decade (IWD), that consciousness has been nurtured and deepened among some segments of the U.S. women's movement. At the mid-decade meeting in Copenhagen, the political and ideological controversies that mark the United Nations disrupted the Conference. The inclusion of Zionism as a form of racism in the final Program of Action split the Conference. Many women decried the so-called "politicization" of the women's agenda, but such politicization should come as no surprise. Women are political and hold very different political and ideological persuasions. Our lives are lived within the political tensions of the world. The question is not whether women's conferences should be political. They are. The question is: can women join in solidarity across national and ideological lines in order to bridge the political and ideological differences that divide the world? Can we become part of the solution to the world's problems?[39]

The 1985 World Conference in Nairobi began to answer that question. To avoid the win-lose approach that characterized the vote in Copenhagen, the official conference at Nairobi adopted a consensus model of decision-making. Controversial issues were hammered out in negotiating groups. It was through this process of negotiating groups, new to U.N. meetings, that women's skill in arriving at agreements and their determination to serve all the women of the world began to show their power and effectiveness. The women delegates and their male colleagues were able to move the conference beyond the cynicism that so often frustrates the U. N. and in the process, had shown women's leadership skills. The global women's movement was coming of age.[40]

The public historic moments of the International Women's Decade— Mexico City, Copenhagen, and Nairobi—created the opportunities for innumerable networks, joint projects, friendships, and struggles for authentic solidarity that continue to shape the global women's movement. Within this global project, the various strands of the U.S. women's movement continue to find both common cause and ideological differences.

First Women's National Conference

Returning from Mexico City, Bella Abzug, former congresswoman from New York, and several other congresswomen led Congress to mandate and fund the First Women's National Conference. The law, PL 94-167, passed late in 1975, was very specific in its provisions. It mandated that the National Commission for IWY convene a National Women's Conference. The Conference was to be preceded by state and regional meetings through which state delegates were to be elected. Furthermore, the delegates were to include representatives of a variety of groups that "work to advance the rights of women," and special emphasis was to be placed on "representatives of low-income women, members of diverse racial, ethnic, and religious groups, and women of all ages."[41] This wording guaranteed the widest possible representation of U.S. women.

During 1976 and 1977, state and territorial meetings were held, delegates elected, and recommendations forwarded to the National Commission. These recommendations formed the basis for the proposed National Plan of Action. The state meetings were often controversial and many became the battleground between feminist and anti-feminist women. Certain religious and traditional opposition forces worked either to take over or to disrupt the process.

The National Conference opened in Houston on November 19, 1977, with 1,403 delegates, 370 delegates-at-large, and 186 alternates, with a sprinkling of men. Thousands of other women and a few men attended as invited guests and observers, watching the Conference from the sidelines and participating in the myriad associated events. The meeting was a continuous celebration of women.[42]

The twenty-six planks of the National Plan of Action were debated and voted upon. The Plan sought to address the variety of needs and experiences reflecting the diversity of women's experience. For the first time in their history the women of the U.S. had a national agenda. The scope of the plan covered the major feminist concerns: Arts and Humanities, Battered Women, Business, Child Abuse, Child Care, Credit, Disabled Women, Education, Elective and Appointive Office, Employment, Equal Rights Amendment, Health, Homemakers, Insurance, International Affairs, Media, Minority Women, Offenders, Older Women, Rape, Reproductive

Freedom, Rural Women, Sexual Preference, Statistics, and Women, Welfare, and Poverty.

The plan was not without controversy. Three planks created major floor struggles: Reproductive Freedom, Sexual Preference and Minority Women. The so-called pro-life forces sought unsuccessfully to block the Reproductive Freedom plank. Lesbian women, who had been struggling since the late 60s to illustrate that lesbian rights were central to women's rights, finally achieved this goal when the National Plan included the Sexual Preference plank.

A high point in the meeting was the moment when Afro-American, Latina, Asian, and Native American women presented an alternative Minority Women's plank. The Conference accepted the alternative plank, and for the first time at a national meeting, women from the minority groups clearly defined their distinct voice, experience, and agenda. The clarity of these voices within the movement has increased in the years that followed.

The opposition forces also gathered at Houston. Within the official meeting, they were massively outnumbered and although they raised their voices in objection to the Plan of Action, they did not attempt to disrupt the meeting. At the end, however, they filed an official minority report addressing each of the planks. These so-called "anti-feminists" had formed a caucus to develop the report, claiming the National Commission and state coordinators had "deliberately excluded or given only token representation to the views of the traditional, family-oriented woman, who has been virtually unrepresented. . . ."[43] A counter-rally of about 10,000 anti-feminists was held across the city. Although the media gave disproportionate coverage to this rally, the press presented a generally positive image of the impressive achievement of the women at the National Conference.[44]

Two structures, one bureaucratic and one organizational, resulted from the Houston event. President Carter established the National Advisory Committee for Women, naming Bella Abzug and Carmen Delgado Votow as co-chairs. The Committee met for two years, but when the co-chairs met with Carter to criticize his budget priorities for 1980, he fired Bella Abzug and virtually told the women to stick to "women's issues." Over half the Committee resigned.[45] Carter appointed new members to the Commission, but its credibility had been destroyed.

The organizational structure which emerged from Houston has had a varied history. It was first established as a rather loose-knit group of some 400 delegates called the Continuing Committee (CC), but it had the almost impossible task of organizing itself and focusing its energies. Finally, in 1981, a small group of women from the CC reorganized themselves as the National Women's Conference Committee (NWCC), and established The National Women's Conference Center as its non-profit, educational/research arm. With a small dedicated membership and no major funding, the NWCC has worked to monitor the National Plan of Action as it is being implemented by women across the states and within the federal government. The NWCC also promotes statewide and regional networks based on the Plan. It is the only group that has attempted to trace and encourage the implementation of the National Plan.[46]

With the election of Ronald Reagan and the ascendancy of the New Right in 1980, feminists returned to the "woodwork" of the bureaucracy. The official U.S. delegation at the U.N. World Conference for Women, Nairobi, 1985, was orchestrated by a clearly conservative approach to both domestic and international issues. The organizational feminists and the "woodwork" feminists cooperated to influence the agenda, but clearly, feminists within the government bureaucracies were no longer in a position to influence major policy directions.

Mainstreaming and Transformation—The 80s

For the most part, the 80s have been a consistent testimony to the work of women during the 70s. The failure of the ERA was a great symbolic loss, celebrated as the death of feminism by the anti-feminists. But it was more a loss of the symbol than a loss of the agenda the symbol represented. That the women's movement has established itself as a significant force in society can be seen by a number of factors.

The changes, so tumultuous in the 60s and early 70s, are today taken for granted. The "new girl" network established during the national and international conferences during the 70s has begun to pay off for women as they move ahead in the business, professional, and political worlds. There is now a corps of talented professionals to act as mentors for younger women entering those fields. Furthermore, women continue to break the "first women" barrier in all parts of society, establishing their competency and paving the way for the women who will follow.

Women's studies programs and research centers are established academic forces on colleges and universities throughout the U.S. Women scholars, informed by the insights of feminist analysis, are doing breakthrough research in all the disciplines, fundamentally rewriting patriarchal knowledge.

Most significantly, a profound shift in consciousness and expectations is becoming evident not only personally among women and men, but societally. These expectations are shared by women and men who would never identify themselves as feminist and never took an active part in the early years of the movement. Few women today expect to live out their lives as homemakers. Most young women expect their future husbands to share in homemaking and childrearing. Many men and women have come to expect a double family income. New models of family life are emerging. Sexist jokes or innuendoes are no longer publicly tolerated. A new ethos of professional, intellectual, and social equality between women and men is emerging. While these changes are neither uniform nor universal, they are evident in growing numbers of women and men. Conservative backlash to these changes is also evident.

More and more women are seeking and winning public office. The nomination of Geraldine Ferraro as the vice-presidential candidate was a high point for women everywhere. Poll takers have identified the "gender gap" in voting patterns. For the first time in history, the women's vote is considered politically significant. In short, the movement and many of its goals have become mainstream. So mainstream, in fact, that many younger women no longer see any need to be part of the women's movement. The gains their foremothers fought so hard to secure are now taken for granted. Young women today, by and large, experience a very different world from young women of twenty-five years ago. In some ways, the movement's very success has deflated its energy.

Certainly, there are still issues to be addressed: child care centers, pay equity, the ERA, economic equity in insurance, pension, and Social Security, enlightened welfare reform, education and socialization of children, medical benefits and housing opportunities, to cite a few. But the organizations are in place and the legitimacy of the questions have been established. It is only the political will that must be activated.

But troubling realities remain. In 1981, the National Advisory Council on Economic Opportunity reported on the "feminization of poverty," a trend first identified by Diana Pearce in 1978.[47] This poverty is located predominately among households headed by women, among women from minority groups in the U.S., and among older women. The majority of women workers still are located in low-paying female-job ghettoes. Over 60% of those on minimum wage are women. Women's poverty shows not only in employment questions but also in housing, medical care, lack of training and education, and in welfare dependency.

As I noted in the Introduction, the abortion issue remains a troubling and unresolved question. No moral consensus has emerged within the society. Family life is under stress financially and emotionally, and women are called upon to be "super-women," successful and assertive in the business world, supportive and nurturing in the home. Adequate child care and senior centers are not available for families with caregiving responsibilities.

In emergency situations, it is still the woman who is expected to respond. The tension between women's traditional work of caregiving in the family and their expanded work in the paid workforce has not been solved.

The question of family life and women's work has become a central issue of the 80s. Betty Friedan, an accurate reader of the social environment, first raised the issue in her book, *The Second Stage*, written in 1981. Sylvia Ann Hewlett's book, *A Lesser Life: The Myth Of Women's Liberation In America*, written in 1986, focused the problem even more and angered many feminists. She outlines her argument and her frustration in the Introduction:

> The problem centers on a clash of roles. Those of us who reached maturity in the 1970s were expected to clone the male competitive model in the labor market while raising our children in our spare time. Compounding this double burden were gratuitous psychological pressures, because we were also expected to raise these children according to wildly inflated notions of motherhood. In essence, I belonged to that "lucky" generation of superwomen who got to combine the nurturing standards of the 1950s with the strident feminism of the 70s. But as many of us discovered when we struggled to bear and raise children mid-career, the rigid standards of the 1950s "cult of motherhood" are impossible to combine with the equally rigid standards of our fiercely competitive workplaces. Mere mortals such as I end up trapped between

the demands of the earth mothers and the hard-nosed careerists, and because these demands are incompatible and contradictory, we are ultimately unable to satisfy either. Neither hired help nor supportive husbands can insulate working mothers from these antagonistic pressures.[48]

Hewlett argues that the U.S. women's movement has failed women because it has not taken seriously the central conflict in women's lives: work and family. The book offers little comfort to either feminist or antifeminist as she excoriates both images of women. But it did succeed in generating some public debate and pointing to the reality that the multiple demands of women's lives raise critical questions not only about current feminist agendas, but about the shape of our human institutions.

Moreover, a deep irony is appearing in the very mainstreaming of the women's movement. As more and more women are moving into full participation as equals in all aspects of our social, political, and economic life, the limitations of the existing systems and structures to respond to women's particular realities are becoming evident. The traditional structures of society are shaped by clearly defined role expectations: men in the public sphere and women in the private or domestic sphere. The structures are not able to respond to women, whose lived experience spans the division between the public and private spheres. As more and more women enter the public sphere, they are discovering that not only have the political, economic, and social structures of modern industrial society traditionally been closed to them as women, but, in fact, these structures are too narrow to accommodate the multiple demands and talents of their lives as women.

Women are discovering that the public domain, traditionally the preserve of men, is in fact alien to women's experience. Unwilling to completely forego their experience and clone themselves into the traditional male experience, some women are questioning the very structures of society.

Such questioning is leading these women to a revaluing of the women's agenda as it has evolved over the last two decades. Have the changes we have struggled for touched the core of patriarchal control of our political, economic, and social structures or have they only opened up a little space for some women to function in those structures? What is the potential for society to regress from the advances women have gained? Is this potential for regression linked to the fact that the changes that have occurred are inadequate solutions to the problems women face in patriarchal structures? Has the women's movement, in concentrating its agenda primarily on the advancement of women, failed to incorporate related issues, such as, for example, the wider economic issues of debt—personal, national, and global—and its impact on the quality of life for all? How has the advancement of some women touched the poverty and marginalization of so many other women?

To answer such questions, the future agenda of the women's movement must move beyond equality toward transformation of our social structures. The charting of a feminist transformative agenda in great measure depends on the analysis of how current structures need to change to accommodate women's reality. That process demands social analysis. Chapter 3 will examine the feminist contribution to the process of social analysis and will describe the various feminist ideologies that shape that analysis.

Process Questions

1. When did you first become aware of the second wave of the women's movement? What were the sources of your information? How did you feel about the movement?

2. What did you find yourself drawn to in the movement? What alienated you? What issues engaged you? What actions did you take? Why?

3. What are your questions for the movement at this time?

Endnotes

1. *The Feminist Papers,* ed. by Alice Rossi (New York: Bantam Books, 1974), pp. 10-11. Original spelling and style retained.

2. Rossi, p. 11. Original spelling and style retained.

3. Josephine Donovan, *Feminist Theory: The Intellectual Traditions of American Feminism* (New York: Frederick Ungar Publishing Co., 1985), p. 17.

4. Rossi, p. 416.

5. The cult of "ideal womanhood" was the nineteenth century's social and cultural response to the violence of the newly emerging Industrial Revolution. The role of the middle-class woman was to provide a haven of peace and security in the home to which the husband could retreat from the viciousness of economic survival.

6. As quoted in Rosemary Radford Ruether, "Home and Work: Women's Roles and the Transformation of Values," in *Women: New Dimensions* ed. by Walter Burghardt, SJ (New York: Paulist Press, 1975), p. 77.

7. Barbara Sinclair Deckard, *The Women's Movement: Political, Socioeconomic and Psychological Issues*, 3rd edition (New York: Harper Row, Publishers, Inc., 1983), p. 284.

8. Alice Kessler-Harris, *Woman Have Always Worked: A Historical Overview* (Old Westbury, New York: The Feminist Press, 1981), p. 93; and Myra Marx Ferree and Beth B. Hess, *Controversy and Coalition: The New Feminist Movement* (Boston: Twayne Publishers, 1985), p. 19.

9. Ferree and Hess, p. 51; and Jo Freeman, *The Politics of Women's Liberation* (New York: David McKay Company, Inc., 1975), pp. 232-234.

10. "...*To Form A More Perfect Union*...": *Justice For American Women*, Report of the National Commission on the Observance of International Women's Year, 1976 (Washington, DC: U.S. Government Printing Office, 1976), p. 6; and Angela Davis, *Woman Race and Class* (New York: Random House, 1981), p. 134.

11. In identifying these historical strands of contemporary feminism, I have drawn upon the work of Ferree and Hess, *Controversy and Coalition: The New Feminist Movement* and Jo Freeman, *The Politics of Women's Organization*. Freeman identifies "two branches" of the movement, an older one and a younger one, each emerging out of a particular set of historical circumstances and differing in age, structure and style. Ferree and Hess identify "two strands of the movement," the bureaucratic and collectivist strands. They prefer the idea of strands rather than branches, since "branches grow apart and remain separate, while strands typically intertwine to produce a particular fabric" (p. 49). I have chosen to use "strands" because my analysis indicates that is the more accurate evolution, but I have chosen to identify three strands of the movement: bureaucratic, organizational and collectivist, dividing the Ferree and Hess strand, "bureaucratic," into bureaucratic and organizational.

12. Deckard, pp. 320-322; and Ferree and Hess, pp. 51-53.

13. Deckard, pp. 322-333; and Ferree and Hess, pp. 52-53.

14. Deckard, p. 324; and Ferree and Hess, pp. 54-55.

15. Freeman, p. 147.

16. Deckard, p. 347.

17. Sara Evans, *Personal Politics: The Roots of Women's Liberation In the Civil Rights Movement and the New Left* (New York: Vintage Books, 1979), p. 37. This book remains one of the best accounts of the experience of women in both the civil rights and the new left movements; an experience that led to the explosion of women's energy in addressing their own liberation. Also see Jo Freeman, *The Politics of Women's Liberation* and Barbara Sinclair Deckard, *The Women's Movement: Political, Socioeconomic and Psychological Issues*.

18. Evans, p. 78.

19. Evans, p. 95.

20. Evans, p. 87.

21. Evans, p. 108.

22. Lydia Sargent, "New Left Women and Men: The Honeymoon is Over," in *Women and Revolution*, ed. by Lydia Sargent (Boston: South End Press, 1981), p. xii.

23. Sargent, p. xiii.

24. Olive Banks, *Faces of Feminism*, (Oxford, UK: Basil Blackwell Ltd., 1981), p. 225; Evans, p. 201; Freeman, p. 59; and Deckard, p. 327.

25. Evans, p. 199; and Freeman, pp. 57ff.

26. Deckard, p. 328.

42 Transforming Feminism

27. Freeman, p. 110; and Deckard, p. 328.

28. Evans, p. 214; Deckard, p. 329; and Ferree and Hess, pp. 61-62. Also see Freeman, p. 148: "The women's liberation movement 'took off' in 1970. It was during that year that the accelerating influx of new people became too great for the groups and organizations to handle, and that new groups were formed more quickly than anyone could keep count. Of great importance in this development was what has been called the 'grand press blitz,' which took place primarily but not exclusively between January and March of that year. Women's liberation became the latest fad. Virtually every major publication and network in the country did a major story on it. While evidence abounds that the media alone does not induce people to make a commitment to a new innovation or a new movement, they do provide information of its existence and to some extent legitimate what would otherwise be seen as an outlandish idea."

29. Freeman, pp. 106-108; Deckard, pp. 329-330; and Banks, p. 227.

30. Deckard, p. 335.

31. Freeman, p. 84.

32. "Caucus Fact Sheet," Congressional Caucus for Women's Issues, Washington, DC, 1986.

33. *Decade of Achievement: 1977-1987—A Project of a Survey Based on the National Plan of Action for Women*, A Project of the National Women's Conference Center, authored and edited by Susanna Downie et al., (Beaver Dam, WI: The National Women's Conference Center, 1988), p. 55.

34. Alice Walker, *In Search of our Mother's Gardens* (New York: Harcourt Brace Jovanovich, Publishers, 1983), p. xi.

35. *Decade of Achievement*, pp. 1-2.

36. See Freeman, pp. 209-221 for a history of the political effort.

37. Ferree and Hess, pp. 127-129; and Freeman, pp. 222-223.

38. "*. . .To Form a More Perfect Union. . .*", pp. 8-9.

39. Maria Riley, *I Am Because We Are* (Washington, DC: Center of Concern, 1985), p. 11.

40. Maria Riley, "Nairobi: The Women's Movement Comes of Age," *Center Focus*, No. 69 (November 1985), p. 4.

41. Public Law 94-167 as quoted in *The Spirit of Houston: An Official Report to the President, The Congress and the People of the United States* (Washington, DC: U.S. Government Printing Office, 1978), p. 10.

42. *Spirit of Houston*, p. 11.

43. *Spirit of Houston*, p. 265.

44. Deckard, p. 376.

45. Deckard, p. 377; and Ferree and Hess, p. 126.

46. *Decade of Achievement*, p. 7.

47. *Final Report* of the National Advisory Council on Economic Opportunity (Washington, DC: U.S. Government Printing Office, 1981), p. 7ff. See also footnote 6, p. 7.

48. Sylvia Ann Hewlett, *The Lesser Life: The Myth of Women's Liberation in America* (New York: William Morrow and Company, Inc., 1986), p. 16.

3

The Maps Were
Out of Date

The maps they gave us were out of date
by years . . .

—Adrienne Rich[1]

In recent years, social analysis has become the popular tool for social transformation. It has moved outside the theoretical world of academia into the pastoral world of social action for a more just society. It has provided specialists and general practitioners alike with a process of examining the key structures of our world: political, economic, sociological and cultural, as well as their historical evolution. It is woven into the process of liberation theology.[2]

It is also gender blind. That is not to say that women are not at times mentioned as examples, but it does mean that women's experience as a lens of analysis is not usually present.

Feminist analysis is extending the process of social analysis by using women's experience as a lens through which to view all social structures. It is incomplete and evolving as women become more and more adept in the process. Like all processes of social analysis, it is not value free. It is informed by various ideological perspectives rooted in the history of the women's movement. Four different perspectives are identifiable: liberal feminism, cultural feminism, radical feminism, and socialist feminism. They find their roots in the distinctive historical strands of the contemporary women's movement. Liberal feminism is the predominant ideology of bureaucratic and organizational strands of feminism as outlined in Chapter Two. Radical feminism and socialist feminism are nurtured primarily through the small group efforts within the collectivist strand of the women's movement. Cultural feminism, evident throughout the various strands of the movements, finds its historical roots in the moral

43

reform movement of the nineteenth and early part of the twentieth centuries.

However, though the historical and intellectual roots of these ideological perspectives may be distinctive, the history of the women's movement over the last 25 years has not only woven together the strands of the movement, it has also brought the ideologies into significant dialogue with each other. As women have cooperated in joint ventures, their particular perspectives have mutually informed and enlarged each other. In effect, the ideologies have been in dialogue, widening the perspectives of all. Furthermore, the agenda and the perspectives have been enriched through dialogue with a variety of challenging voices: the voices of women who by and large have not been part of the dominant women's movement in the U.S.—so-called "minority women," Afro-American, Latina, Asian American, Native American women, international women, and conservative women.

In this chapter I will examine the distinctive process of feminist analysis and identify the particular contributions each of the ideological perspectives brings to our understanding of the role of gender in social structures. The conclusion of the chapter will include the challenging voices and point to some of the questions and contradictions in contemporary feminism that arise from the different ideological perspectives.

Feminist Analysis

Personal experience rather than theory is the starting point of all feminist analysis. In the beginning, the groups of women who broke from the new left and the civil rights movements engaged in a process they called "consciousness-raising." Patterned on the Chinese practice of "bitter speaking," the women would gather in small groups to tell their stories. These sessions, however, quickly moved beyond merely venting anger and frustration at the experience of oppression to become a process of analysis. Consciousness-raising involves four steps: 1) a period of time when women tell their stories and engage in "active listening" to each other; 2) a shift from storytelling to analysis as the women begin to identify patterns of oppression emerging from their experiences; 3) a recognition that these patterns become the basis for a gender analysis of the social structures that shape our lives; and 4) an understanding that marginalization of women in social structures is linked to other theories of oppression.[3] In the early days of the women's liberation movement, radical feminists used consciousness-raising as a tool for organizing as well as a process for analysis. However, it soon became a common process among all feminists.[4]

Feminism's most radical insight into the process of social analysis is the understanding that the "personal is political." The simplest definition for this insight would state that the structures of a society are "identical in both public and private areas, that what happens in the bedroom has everything to do with what happens in the boardroom, and vice versa, and that mythology notwithstanding, at present the same sex is in control in both places."[5] Or to put it more succinctly: "it is a demand to recognize men's power and women's subordination as both a social and a political reality."[6] This insight, first articulated by radical feminists, has become the foundation of all feminist analysis.

To understand that the personal is political gives feminists a lens to identify links between violence toward women and other forms of violence: violence toward nature, the violence of war. It challenges the artificial distinction between the public and private sphere. It illustrates that the power dynamics that exist between women and men in personal relationships mirror the power dynamics that exist between women and men in the social structures. It gives language to the intuition many women have that "all is connected."

Identifying the personal as political also provides women with a perspective on the process—also called the praxis—of personal and political change. Feminism as a mode of analysis relies on the idea that we come to know the world, to change it and be changed by it, through our everyday activities.[7] But feminism also recognizes that as women become conscious of their reality and begin to redefine themselves, they are integrally engaged in political change. As Sandra Harding succinctly states, "We do not act in a vacuum to produce and reproduce our lives; changed consciousness and changed definitions of self can occur only in conjunction with restructuring the social (societal and personal) relationships in which each of us is involved. . . . We can transform ourselves only by simultaneously struggling to transform the social relations that define us: self-changing and changed social institutions are simply two aspects of the same process."[8] The symbiosis between personal and political transformation is the basis of feminist praxis. Chris Williamson, a feminist musician and composer, captured this understanding in her widely popular album *The Changer and the Changed.*

Ideological Perspectives

Feminism as we understand it today is a rich and complex blend of ideas, histories, and ideological perspectives.* Each ideological perspective, beginning from its particular vantage point of analysis, makes a unique contribution to our understanding of the place of gender in social structures. Liberal feminism analyzes the place of women primarily from a legal/political perspective. Cultural feminism identifies the power of women. Radical feminism focuses its analysis on the culture of patriarchy. Socialist feminism raises economic and class questions. Each carries a specific agenda for change arising from its particular analysis.

Finally, it is important to reiterate that these different ideological perspectives continue to shape and reshape each other within the dynamism of the women's movement. In the analyses that follow, I will briefly outline the contributions each of the ideologies brings to our understanding of women's reality. These analyses do not describe individual feminists; they are about the intellectual foundations that shape and reshape the perspectives of women and men seeking social change.

Liberal Feminism

Liberal feminism has its intellectual roots in that extraordinary philosophic, political, and economic ferment of the eighteenth century called the Age of Enlightenment. Out of that ferment the foundations of modern society in the Western world were spawned: liberalism, democracy and capitalism. The United States is one of the great experiments in those ideas.

The fundamental belief of liberalism is in the common and universal nature of all human persons. Rationality is the defining characteristic of the human. This idea was not new to western thought, but when Rene Descartes, the central philosopher of the age, wrote his famous line, "I think, therefore I am," he identified rationality as the sole defining and individuating characteristic of human nature. He also reinforced the body-mind

---

*See Appendix B for graphic summary of contemporary feminism.

dualism of some strains of Western philosophic thought. By identifying thinking as the defining act for human existence, Descartes set up the individual's conscience as the first and final judge of truth and morality. He was also laying the foundation for a social philosophy which holds that the highest good is the freedom of the individual from external constraints, either from the church or the state. The role of government is to protect individual freedom.

These emphases pave the way for a type of radical individualism which claims personal independence as the fundamental right. The only universal moral norm is that the exercise of personal rights should not interfere with the rights of others. This norm sets up the distinction between the private and the public domains in society. The "right to privacy," a personal right, governs the private domain. Government is neither to interfere nor to impose standards or regulations within the private sphere. The role of the state is to regulate the public domain only in order to protect the rights and independence of all citizens.

Furthermore, because we all share a common human nature, we also share the same (equal) civil, political, and legal rights. However, we do not share equal economic rights. The economy is ruled by the supply and demand of the market place, the arena in which the free individuals of the liberal capitalistic tradition seek their individual destinies. The market reflects the complex interaction of individuals' self-interest, an essential element in human nature. Governments should protect the freedom of all individuals to pursue their interests, not try to control them even for the sake of some well-intentioned social goal.

Liberalism set the philosophic framework for both laissez-faire capitalism and democracy as the ideal egalitarian political-economic environment where individuals could pursue personal autonomy and self-fulfillment with the least possible interference. The ringing words of the Declaration of Independence are a paean of praise to a liberal order of society: "We hold these truths to be self-evident, that all men [sic] are created equal, that they are endowed by their Creator with certain unalienable Rights, that among these are Life, Liberty, and the pursuit of Happiness. That to secure these rights, Governments are instituted among Men, [sic] deriving their just powers from the consent of the governed."[9]

The American dream was born. However, history reveals that in reality, the dream only applied to white, property-owning males. The reality of

U.S. history has been one long struggle of blacks, minority groups and women within the U.S. to achieve equal rights with white men. The struggles themselves are beginning to reveal the inadequacies of the liberal view of social order.

Liberal feminism appropriates the 18th century doctrine of common human nature with equal rights and applies it to women. The Seneca Falls Declaration of 1848 pointedly opens with a paraphrase of the Declaration of Independence: "We hold these truths to be self-evident: that all men and women are created equal. . . ."[10] The civil rights movement of the 1960s was another expression of the struggle to extend these rights to Afro-Americans.

Liberal feminism focuses its analysis on the historical exclusion of women from access to and equal rights in the traditional spheres where men hold power and control access: politics, economics, religion, education, culture. The goal of liberal feminism is twofold: 1) to dismantle the historical structures of patriarchal law that deny women full legal, political, economic, and civil rights as autonomous adults; and 2) to achieve equal access to all structures of society—political, economic, social, and cultural.

Liberal feminism is the most pervasive feminist ideology in the U.S. because it is so rooted in the foundational American ideology. Historically, the bureaucratic and organizational strands of the women's movement are the primary carriers of liberal feminism. The results of their efforts are impressive. Despite the failure of the Equal Rights Amendment (ERA), a fundamental liberal tenet, liberal feminism has made significant impact on both public policy and public awareness over the past 25 years. The image and role of woman in society is changing. Using traditional political tactics such as lobbying, letter-writing campaigns, testimony at hearings, demonstrations and legal suits, liberal feminists have successfully used the system to advance women's equality in significant ways. But full equality in all our systems and structures has not yet been achieved.

Economic equity remains the goal of the 80s and 90s. The issues include pension reform, tax reform, insurance reform, property rights, pay equity, equal access to credit, as well as Social Security and welfare reform. Equal opportunity remains a cornerstone of liberal feminism. Because education and training give access to equal opportunity in the work place, education has always been a primary concern for liberal feminists. In the nineteenth century, the struggle was guaranteeing women's rights to enter schools. The twentieth century agenda has been to guarantee equal opportunities within the educational institutions. Title IX of the Education Act (1972) protects women from unequal treatment in admissions requirements, programs, facilities, financial aid, and student health benefits. Efforts also extend to gaining access to equal training opportunities and jobs, particularly jobs that have been traditionally closed to women.

Recognizing that women's traditional roles in the private sphere as mother and homemaker have placed her at a disadvantage in the public work place, liberal feminism has emphasized the need for child care, for women's right to reproductive freedom and for maternity/paternity leave. It is at this juncture between the private and the public, however, that liberalism fails to address the complexity of women's experience.

The demands of women's traditional work in the so-called private world continue to overflow into the so-called public world. This dualism between the private and public spheres which has been set up by liberal philosophy creates artificial lives for many women. While working outside the home, many women are still called upon to be totally responsible for both daily and emergency tasks that surround their families. The value of and responsibility for relationships in women's lives keep challenging the liberal ideal of the independent autonomous individual.[11]

However, women owe a great deal to the liberal tradition. It has held the promise of equality, human dignity, and self-fulfillment.[12] Liberal feminism has led the way in removing many barriers to women's full participation in society. Ironically, its very successes have begun to reveal the limitations of the liberal tradition as an adequate framework for women's experience, and therefore, as an adequate framework for human experience.

Process Questions

1. What is the meaning of equality in liberal feminism? Equal to what standard? Who sets it?

2. What do you think are liberal feminism's most important contributions to the women's movement?

3. What questions would you raise concerning liberal feminism?

4. What does the liberal feminist's lens of analysis fail to see?

Cultural Feminism

Cultural feminism[13], also called romantic or moral reform feminism, has its roots in the nineteenth century moral reform movements. Its most popular current expression is the song "Bread and Roses" which feminists sing with much gusto: ". . . the rising of the women means the rising of the race." It is based on two premises: 1) the natural moral superiority of women and 2) the need for that moral superiority to take shape in public policy.

The influence of cultural feminism is subtle and extensive not only within the women's movement, but also throughout the larger society. It appears not only in progressive, change-oriented groups, but also among conservative groups. For example, a common perspective within parts of the peace community is "women are the peace makers." This perspective was also apparent in a remark of former President Ronald Reagan that if it weren't for women, men would still be wearing animal skins and carrying clubs.

Cultural feminism grew within the social and economic realities of the beginning stages of industrial capitalism in the early nineteenth century. It was a reaction against the ruthlessness of the era and its calloused position of social darwinism—the survival of the economically fittest. Patriarchy responded to that reality by developing the cult of "ideal womanhood." The role of woman was to provide a haven of peace and harmony within the home to which man could come to escape the harshness of the marketplace. Feminists responded by accepting their role of moral superriority. They then struggled to bring their superior moral vision both to social relations and to the public order. In some ways, cultural feminism can be called "women's revenge" on the patriarchal dogma of the "cult of ideal womanhood" that dominated nineteenth century social mores.[14]

Early cultural feminism held out a "matriarchal vision: the idea of a society of strong women guided by essentially female concerns and values."[15] These values were rooted in women's contribution to the creation of strong family life. The concerns and values included morality, pacifism, and social welfare as well as the introduction of "feminine traits" into the larger culture. Cultural feminism identified the male culture as aggressive, competitive, rationalistic, detached, despotic. In contrast, women's culture was harmonious, intuitive, emotional, natural, holistic, shaped by special moral sensibilities. Within this view, the women's rights movement was seen not as an end in itself but as a means to bring about larger social and cultural reform.[16]

The agenda of cultural feminism included the abolition of the double moral standard for women and men, especially in sexual mores. However, the goal was not the so-called "sexual revolution" as we understand it in the twentieth century, when the advent of effective birth control opened the way for greater sexual freedom for women. Rather, cultural feminism called for men to adopt the standards that women traditionally held and were held to.[17]

Defending the weak in society became a primary concern as cultural feminism struggled to extend "feminine" values into the public order. Its agenda included the protection of children, especially against the abusive labor systems; the protection of family life through such means as the temperance crusade; the development of the social welfare system to alleviate the human suffering caused by the cruelties of social darwinism; and the pursuit of peace through the harmonious resolution of conflict.[18]

The answer to the question of whether these so-called feminine values are a result of nature or nurture has a varied history. Early cultural feminism argued that women and men were naturally different, and extended biological differences to include psychological and moral differences. Contemporary cultural feminism would accept the concept that women are socialized or nurtured to develop certain characteristics. Carol Gilligan's work, *In A Different Voice*, is a modern classic in developing the thesis that women do perceive and respond to events differently; however, this difference is a result of women's particular development process.[19] Both radical feminism and socialist feminism agree strongly that women are a product of their social conditioning. However, some conservative women today would be closer to the early cultural feminists.

Today, cultural feminism advocates that women's political ideology be derived from women's traditional culture and be applied to public issues.[20] It seeks not only a political transformation, but more importantly, a cultural transformation. It promotes women in mutual partnership with men in all spheres of human activity as the process whereby women's culture and values will be diffused throughout society.

Cultural feminism lacks an analytical framework for understanding women's place in social structures. It is also based on the romantic, highly questionable thesis of women's moral superiority to men. However, it finds a comfortable home in both progressive and conservative circles, and therefore operates as one of the most enduring ideologies of feminism.

Process Questions

1. What do you agree with in cultural feminism?
2. Do you question any of its tenets? Why?
3. What does the lens of cultural feminism fail to see?

Radical Feminism

Radical feminism is a uniquely twentieth century ideology. It developed as a revolt against the political theories, experiences, structural forms, and personal style of both the new left movement and the civil rights movement of the 1960s. Its fundamental premise and invaluable contribution to our understanding of social structures is the principle already mentioned in this chapter, that the "personal is political." It insists that personal, "subjective" issues, especially between women and men, are as important and legitimate as other social issues—war, peace, poverty, racism, ecological destruction. In fact, radical feminism insists, the root—radical—cause of all these issues is the primary pattern of men's domination of women.[21]

Radical feminism offers a comprehensive and trenchant analysis of the culture of patriarchy and how it shapes and controls not only all social structures but also personal relationships. In fact, because of the very comprehensiveness of its analysis, there is no single coherent statement of radical feminism that gathers its multiple and varied analyses as they are continuously being articulated by different radical feminist groups. However, two main activities characterize radical feminism: 1) the analysis of the culture of patriarchy; and 2) the development of an alternative feminist culture.[22]

The central issue in the radical feminist analysis of patriarchy is men's control of women. That control is manifest above all in the subordination of women's bodies, sexuality and reproductive capacity by male ownership. This control includes patriarchal religion's practice of defining the morality of women's sexuality and reproductive capacity. All other forms of male control are related to this primary control of women's bodies.

According to radical feminist analysis, patriarchy demands hierarchy—the system in which one group—men—is considered more important, more valuable, more notable than another group—women—who are therefore rightfully subordinate, passive, dependent. Early feminists identified the politics of patriarchy as the "politics of ego," arguing that the primary cause of male domination is the male need for psychological ego satisfaction through dominating women.[23] Later radical feminism extends the politics of patriarchy to include not only psychological control but also political, religious, sexual, economic, cultural, and social control.

In analyzing the structures of this pervasive control, radical feminism has challenged some of our most cherished and traditional institutions—family structure, romantic love, personal relationships, the self-identity of women and men. Radical feminism accepts the common sociological distinction between sex and gender. Sex is the biological distinction between female and male. Gender is the socially engineered roles and characteristics known as masculine and feminine. While celebrating women's sexuality, radical feminism condemns all forms of patriarchy and hierarchy because they structure gender subordination of women in all social systems and personal relationships.

It has also exposed the violent means used to control women: rape, domestic violence, incest, pornography. It sees all of these realities as different expressions of the same problem: men seeking to dominate women personally and structurally. It includes racism, war, torture, the destruction of the environment, and the rape of the land as further manifestations of this will to dominate.

To illustrate this thesis, radical feminism points to both ancient laws and modern practices. In ancient law, women were considered the property of their fathers and then of their husbands. A remnant of that law remains today in traditional wedding ceremonies where the bride is "given away" by her father to her husband.

Because women were considered property of men, rape was traditionally considered a crime against the father, the husband or the family, not an act of violence forced upon a woman. It has only been in recent years, after innumerable and painful legal and social struggles by feminists, that women are beginning to realize that rape is a crime against them, not something for which they should take blame and hide from their families and society. The difficulty of these struggles reveals the power that cultural expectations exert on us. Rape victims often feel the guilt of a temptress or of an unfaithful wife rather than the just rage of a violated victim.

Moreover, the patriarchal culture maintains a kind of psychological control over women by enforcing a dual image of women: the maternal woman to nurture and care for men, and the sexual woman to fulfill men's fantasies and physical needs. Mary and Eve, the mother and the temptress, the faithful wife and the whore. Between these two images, women are separated from each other and separated from themselves.

Radical feminism theorizes that the institution of the patriarchal family arose over the issue of inheritance rights. Men had to control the fertility of their wives to insure that the children born were "legitimate" and therefore rightful heirs of the *patri*mony [emphasis mine]. In the patriarchal world, no such control is demanded over the men's reproductive capacities. Furthermore, radical feminism argues that all patriarchal social and religious institutions conspired to enforce that control, until today we live in a culture where "sex class is so deep as to be invisible."[24]

The question of motherhood is a central lens of analysis for radical feminism. It is analyzed as both negative and positive in women's experience.

Negatively, the cult of motherhood is seen as a means of controlling and subordinating women. Under patriarchy, women are identified not as individual persons, but through their functions and relationships, the primary function and relationship being motherhood. From earliest childhood, women are prepared and directed by cultural mores, social imperatives, patriarchal family structures, and educational processes to envision their future as devoted wives and ideal mothers. The programming is so pervasive that women themselves come to believe that their primary function is motherhood and, to accept themselves as subordinated to and dependent upon men.

However, motherhood is also seen as a positive experience within radical feminist thought because it is the basis for the theory of two cultures: patriarchal culture and the alternative women's culture. Patriarchal culture, built on a structure of domination and subordination, is by its very nature violent: overtly violent in such acts as rape, pornography, woman battering, torture, war, ecological destruction; and covertly violent in such acts as exclusion, psychological diminishment, detached rationality, economic dependency, imposed limitations. Women's culture, on the contrary, formed as it has been by the traditional role of motherhood, is characterized as nurturing, close to nature, compassionate, intuitive, open, flexible. It is also non-dualistic, not separating intuition from thought, emotion from reason, body from spirit, nature from culture. This women's culture, submerged within the dominant patriarchal culture, is the basis for a "feminist future."

Celebrating and developing women's culture is the second major contribution of radical feminism to our understanding of social structures. Women artists, musicians, writers, poets, women's collectives, women's economic enterprises, health clinics, book stores, restaurants, women's shelters, rape crisis centers,—the list is wide and continues to show the creativity and variety of radical feminism. Central to this activity is the effort to create "women's space" within a patriarchal world: space for women to explore their own needs, desires, values, and styles, and to encourage each other, in the living out of their experience as women. Characteristically, women's culture consciously seeks to develop and to illustrate new non-hierarchical structures and new non-linear modes of thought and styles of expression. Because its agenda, to celebrate and to develop women's culture, is so extensive, radical feminism embraces a multiplicity of issues, interests and traditions, from peace and ecology to Zen and astrology, to covens and goddesses, in its search for and re-creation of women's culture.

Participation in these women-directed and women-defined enterprises creates a two-fold form of feminist political action: 1) women withdraw their support from dominant male-directed and male-defined structures, and 2) they create a new culture which is radically subversive within the dominant culture. Radical feminism and cultural feminism are the only ideologies that deny the subtle but pervasive position that the male experience is normative for the human experience. Radical feminism enters both the process of analysis and the process of celebrating women's culture consciously as women. This is a profoundly important contribution to our understanding of human nature. However, in being so consciously woman-focused, it is often perceived as being anti-male.

Some radical feminism is clearly separatist, that is, it is exclusively female in both analysis and action. Lesbianism within the movement is twofold: it is political and it is personal. Politically, lesbianism is a challenge to patriarchal culture's norm of "compulsory heterosexuality." It challenges the traditional model of male-defined women with the reality of women-defined-women. It differs from the gay world in its clear political agenda and action against patriarchy. Personally, lesbianism is also a lifestyle and, in many cases, a life commitment. Some lesbian analysis insists that lesbian separateness is the only authentic form of feminism, following the logic of the radical feminist analysis. However, not all radical feminists are separatists. Nor are all lesbians feminists.

Radical feminism as we know it today is truly a twentieth century development. Its goal is the liberation of women from all male control: a goal that could not have been imagined before the twentieth century with the advent of reproductive technology and the potential for women to be economically independent. Its contribution to feminist analysis is its piercing understanding of patriarchal cultural and its celebration of women's cult-However, it often ignores other oppressions women endure, such as racism or economic classism.

Process Questions

1. What do you think radical feminism's most important contributions are?

2. What do you agree with in radical feminist analysis?

3. What questions do you raise about radical feminism?

4. What does the radical feminist lens of analysis fail to see?

Socialist Feminism

Socialist feminism is a hybrid theory which seeks to combine the best insights of radical feminism with the best insights of marxism in order to avoid the limitations of both. It emerged in the early 1970s as the ideological perspective of the women who were active in both the new left and the early radical feminist movements. Socialist feminism developed after the early ideological rupture in radical feminism at a meeting in Chicago in

1968. The radical feminists insisted that the primary problem was patriarchy; socialist feminists, schooled in the new left's ideology and political action, insisted that women's subordination was part of a wider political agenda.[26] Socialist feminism offers the most coherent analysis of women's subordination.

With some of its theoretical roots in post-marxian thought[27] and in radical feminist thought, socialist feminism challenges both by insisting on questions of class as well as gender in its theory of oppression. While recognizing the central role of patriarchy in oppressing women, socialist feminism faults radical feminism's tendency to universalize women's oppression under the single problem of patriarchy. It criticizes radical feminism for failing to recognize class, race, and historical circumstances in its analysis of women's oppression. Likewise, it challenges marxism for its failure to recognize its own patriarchy, not only in its analytical categories, but also in the political structures of leftist organizations.

Socialist feminism also challenges liberal feminism's equal rights agenda for its abstract ideal of human freedom guaranteed by law, but not rooted in the particular experiences of women. It argues that equal rights are useless if women do not have the economic means to enjoy them. Without economic independence, education, property, and professional positions remain a privilege of class.

Socialist feminism and radical feminism are by far the most revolutionary expressions of the women's movement, and question not only women's subordinate position in all existing structures and systems, but also the very legitimacy of those structures and systems as they presently exist.[28]

Positively, socialist feminism seeks to develop and articulate a comprehensive theory of women's oppression. It also attempts to bridge the dispute on political priorities that periodically erupts within the women's liberation movement. Should the women's struggle for liberation be subordinated to the class struggle or to the struggle against racism? Or does the struggle against patriarchy take precedence over all other struggles? Socialist feminism attempts to avoid such either/or positions, setting out to develop new sets of political and economic categories that show that all forms of domination—sexism, racism, classism and imperialism—are inextricably connected. For socialist feminists, true liberation of the human community demands that all these expressions of domination be abolished.

The central lens of socialist feminism's analysis of women's subordination is the sexual division of labor. Historically, in most Western industrial societies the sexual division of labor has been drawn along biological lines. Women are responsible for reproduction, which is part of the private sphere; men are responsible for production in the public sphere. In this context, reproduction includes not only childbearing, but also childrearing, the myriad tasks of family maintenance, and cultural/psychological socialization. Production includes all forms of work necessary to a functioning society: farming, industry, marketing, law, medicine, government, the arts, and so forth.

Women's work in reproduction is considered natural, rooted in biological realism and familial relationships. It is not understood as economically productive. Part of the ideology of patriarchy insists that women's work is an act of love, not economics. Men's work is economic, constituting the GNP (Gross National Product). Women's entering the public realm of production does not essentially alter our understanding and structuring of this sexual division of labor; it simply involves women in both spheres. Nor does it illumine the complex relationship between the two spheres as they are structured by patriarchy and capitalism. To unmask the patriarchy controlling both spheres is to understand that "the sexual division of labor is not just a division *between* procreation and 'production': it is also a division *within* procreation and *within* 'production' " [emphasis in original].[29]

In analyzing the division of labor within reproduction, socialist feminism relies significantly upon radical feminism's insight that women's subordination is rooted in patriarchy's need to control female sexuality.

One result of this subordination is that the economic base of women's reproductive work has been rendered invisible and unaccounted. Socialist feminism extends this radical feminist insight by identifying female sexual subordination in historical material categories, linking it to the economics of women's work. It accepts and enlarges Shulamith Firestone's original analysis in *The Dialectic of Sex*. She argued that women's reproductive work is the economic foundation of patriarchy; socialist feminism includes both women's reproductive and productive work as the economic foundation of patriarchy.[30]

While recognizing that women's work, both productive and reproductive, changes significantly according to historical and economic circumstances, socialist feminism also seeks to identify a commonality across these historical and economic differences. For example, women are almost universally responsible not only for childbearing and childrearing, but also for maintaining the family in all its needs: food, health care for the young and old, cleanliness, order, and the fostering of loving and sustaining relationships. This sexual division of labor frees men to pursue their control over the public sphere, rendering women's work, which sustains male independence, invisible. It also leaves women economically dependent upon men.

Recognizing that these family needs are essential human needs which must be met, socialist feminism denies that women are biologically determined to meet them for the human family. Rather, it asserts that any historical method for meeting human needs is a matter of social organization and conditioning, and is, therefore, subject to analysis and open to forms of social transformation. The question then emerges: How are we to analyze the interaction between patriarchy and any given social system? Socialist feminist analysis as developed within the U.S. focuses on that interaction within advanced industrial capitalism.

Socialist feminism understands patriarchy as a set of social relationships among men, supported and maintained by their control over women's labor power. Although a system of hierarchy exists among men of different races and classes within patriarchy, it nevertheless creates an interdependence and solidarity among them that enables them to dominate women. Within the patriarchal system, all men are united in their shared relationship of dominance over women.[31] While some men may not choose to exercise their dominance, structurally they enjoy the fruits of a system that relies upon unpaid or underpaid women's labor both in their private lives and in their public work lives.

This system of control and privilege rests on the ideology of men's superiority and women's dependency, economically, socially, and personally.

This ideology is perpetuated by patriarchal institutions—legal, economic, social, educational, and religious—which socialize women and men, girls and boys into their appropriate roles: men to be aggressive and competitive in the profit-driven marketplace; women to be dependent, passive and responsive to the needs of the family, to men and to the demand for low-skilled, low-paying service work needed within the public sector.

When a woman's work is completely within the family unit, she is economically dependent upon the paid work of the man. This dependency becomes all too clear in the case of divorce, abandonment, or sudden death of the husband. In fact, such events do not so much make women poor, as current wisdom would have it, as they reveal how poor and economically dependent women are in their own right.

Women's productive work in the marketplace is usually circumscribed by job and wage/salary ghettos. Current statistics to the contrary, the majority of women are still considered a secondary work force, for two reasons: 1) their primary work is supposed to be homemaking and family maintenance; and 2) their income is considered supplemental to the income of the man. These reasons are used to justify women's disadvantaged position in the marketplace. They also continue to foster that disadvantage.

These dual work-demands, in the private and public sectors, continue to structure women into dependent and inferior positions both in the home and in the marketplace. The lower wages most women are able to command in the workplace perpetuate men's economic advantage over them and encourage women to choose marriage and homemaking as a career, thereby insuring their economic dependency. In turn, women's home responsibilities reinforce their inferior labor market position.[32] According to socialist feminism, women are caught in the dual bind of the ideologies of patriarchy and capitalism. Women's work not only sustains the structures of modern industrial capitalism, it also sustains male dominance. Men also sustain women, but at the price of women's economic dependency and loss of self-determination.

This structural analysis of women's work presents a serious critique of both the split between the public/private spheres as defined by liberalism and the productive/reproductive categories as defined by marxism. By showing that these realms are integrally related in women's experience, socialist feminism reveals that neither liberalism nor marxism is an adequate theory for understanding women's reality. Women's work bridges and encompasses the dualities between public/private and production/reproduction.

Therefore, from the socialist feminist point of view, liberation for women is envisioned as reproductive freedom and economic independence. But both of these need to be understood within the particular perspective of socialist feminism.

Reproductive freedom within this world view goes well beyond liberal feminism's "right to choose." By insisting that reproduction is not solely an individual or private decision but also a social concern, socialist feminism asserts the social and political implications of personal decisions, and vice versa. Children are not viewed only as the personal responsibility of the nuclear family, but are also the responsibility of the society as a whole. They are not the property of their parents, but future citizens of the society. Therefore, society should have some influence over the decision to have or not to have a child, and concomitantly, society has a responsibility to insure the well being of that child.[33]

Furthermore, socialist feminism identifies the various ways that women are denied genuine control over their reproductive lives. These restraints include legal and economic restrictions on the availability of contraception and abortion, forced sterilization, usually upon minority and poor women, lack of support for children of poor women, and the constraints that poverty places on some women's desire to have children.[34] The idea of reproductive freedom includes the freedom to choose to have a child as well as the freedom to choose not to have a child.

The kind of reproductive freedom that socialist women envision would demand a structural change both in social relationships between women and men and in the organization of society. Public and universal concern for child care would be a primary focus of any such restructuring. The responsibility for child care would be separated from gender roles: Men and women would be equally responsible for the care of children, and for the reproduction and production of a society.[35]

Furthermore, society must assume its responsibility to create the context for true reproductive freedom. The context would include providing the necessary material support to provide a true alternative for all people. This support would include safe and available means of birth control, good quality publicly-funded health services, including pre-natal, maternal and pediatric care, publicly-funded and community-controlled child care, as well as safe environments both at work and home, and the provision of adequate jobs, incomes, housing, and education.

In addition, socialist feminism envisions fundamental changes in our process of socializing women and men to certain roles, thus freeing women from "compulsory motherhood" to allow them to develop their capacities in other areas.[36] It envisions a variety of alternatives to current child rearing practices, including communal homes, gay and lesbian families, and extended families, in addition to the nuclear family. Obviously, this vision of reproductive freedom would require a radical restructuring of society and of human relationships.

Economic independence is the second pole supporting the socialist feminist agenda for women's liberation. Achieving economic independence is integrally linked to achieving reproductive freedom. Women often find themselves at a disadvantage in the marketplace because of the present social organization of reproduction and childrearing, as well as the historical control that men have had over public life. In order to allow women equal opportunities in the public work place, accommodations of traditional work patterns need to become part of public policy. One major need is for adequate maternity/paternity leave policy, as well as variations and flexibility in work hours for both men and women. As long as women are regarded as having two roles in society, productive and reproductive, while men have only one, women will find themselves at a disadvantage.[37]

There are other issues to be corrected within the workplace to ensure women's economic independence. The first, obviously, relates to differences that exist in value placed on certain work according to who performs that work, a woman or a man. Differences in the wages/salaries between women and men need to be eliminated. Sexual harassment of women in the work place must be stopped. Women need to be organized in unions and other forms of organization in order to begin to identify their rights as workers and to use collective action to effect change.

Socialist feminism has added intellectual rigor and structural analysis to our understanding of women's reality. Seeking a society where women and men of all classes have the same opportunities to be active parents and to be gainfully employed, it situates women's liberation at the center of all social reform. It also illustrates that there can be no real liberation for women outside of major social reform.

At present, socialist feminism offers the most comprehensive approach to understanding women's reality. But in so doing, it has revealed an extraordinarily complex world that will defy easy solutions both to the struggle for women's liberation beyond patriarchy and to society's movement beyond poverty and injustice. Its analysis challenges not only patriarchy and capitalism, but also less comprehensive theories of feminism and socialism. It has raised the major structural and personal questions; the future directions for truly liberating social changes are still the unfinished agenda.

Process Questions

1. What do you see as socialist feminism's most important contributions to our understanding of women's reality?

2 What do you agree with in socialist feminist analysis?

3. What questions do you raise about socialist feminism?

4. What does the socialist feminist lens of analysis fail to see?

Challenging Voices

"Ain't I a Woman?" Sojourner Truth asked the Second Annual Women's Rights Convention in Akron, Ohio, 1851. With her ringing words she not only challenged the men present who were ridiculing women as dependent and weak creatures, she also challenged the white women to recognize their racism. Although many of the women present were active in the anti-slavery campaigns, they were not at the same time, as subsequent history shows, advocating social equality with the Afro-Americans.[38] More blatant and overt in the nineteenth century, more subtle and hidden in the twentieth, racism has prevailed in the women's movement in the U.S. since its beginning.[39]

The challenge of racism within the movement has been difficult for women from the dominant white culture to acknowledge, but it has come from all quarters: Afro-American women, Latina women, Jewish women, Native American women, Asian American women.[40] It is fundamentally a challenge of accountability. At a talk given at the closing session of the National Women's Studies Association Conference, 1979, Barbara Smith defined the content of this accountability: "The reason racism is a feminist issue is easily explained by the inherent definition of feminism. Feminism is the political theory and practice that struggles to free *all* women: women of color, working-class women, poor women, disabled women, lesbians, old women—as well as white, economically privileged, heterosexual women. Anything less than this vision of total freedom is not feminism, but merely female self-aggrandizement."[41] The challenge has not changed since 1851.

Fundamental to this challenge is a serious questioning of the dominant white feminist analysis of causes of women's oppression. Liberal feminism's primary emphasis is that women's oppression can be alleviated by obtaining equality before the law. Cultural feminism, with its romantic notion of women's moral superiority, lacks a structural analysis of women's oppression. Radical feminism defines the oppression of women as the root structural oppression. Socialist feminism understands patriarchy as a set of social relationships among men, supported and maintained by their control over women's labor power. It recognizes a system of hierarchy among men drawn along race and class lines, but argues that the common goal of the control of women unites all men beyond race and class.

Women who are not of the dominant white culture refute these analyses as inadequate reflections of the U.S. reality. Bell Hooks writes:

> Despite the predominance of patriarchal rule in American society, America was colonized on a racially imperialistic base and not on a sexually imperialistic base. No degree of patriarchal bonding between white male colonizers and Native American men over-shadowed white racial imperialism. Racism took precedence over sexual alliances in both the white world's interaction with Native Americans and African Americans, just as racism overshadowed any bonding between black women and white women on the basis of sex. . . . While those feminists who argue that sexual imperialism is more endemic to all societies than racial imperialism are probably correct, American society is one in which racial imperialism supercedes sexual imperialism.[42]

She continues this analysis by observing that "white racial imperialism granted all white women, however victimized by sexist oppression they might be, the right to assume the role of oppressor in relationship to black women and black men."[43]

As white women in the movement have become more and more sensitive to this criticism and tried to respond to it, the depth of racism within our social fabric and therefore woven through the dominant women's movement has become even clearer. Many women from different races are committed to women's liberation,[44] but that liberation must include their liberation from the oppression of racism, women and men alike. They point out that current feminist analysis, while claiming to be universal, in reality addresses white women's experience. The myopia of white feminism cannot be addressed by simply inviting women from different races and economic backgrounds to be part of its movement. One charge against that invitation is tokenism. A deeper charge, however, points to the fundamental inadequacy of the analysis and the agenda for dealing with the racism within the movement and within society—and therefore its fundamental inadequacy for the liberation of all women.

Language with its power to reveal basic assumptions unmasks some of the problems. Black feminists point out several examples. In the U.S., the white population continues to refer to people of different races as minority groups. They are minority groups only within the Western world. Worldwide, caucasians are the minority.

White women, having defined the directions of the women's movement, continue to invite other women to join "their" movement, adopt their agendas, accept their analysis. Many feminist writers like to make the comparison of women as a minority group with blacks as a minority group. However, a close examination of their language reveals that the word "women" really refers to white women and the word "blacks" usually refers to black men.[45] Black women are subsumed under the group of black men. This linguistic analysis is reflected in the title of the book, *All The Women Are White, All The Blacks Are Men, But Some Of Us Are Brave.*[46]

The current, common use of the word "Hispanic" is another example. Most persons whom the U.S. society places under that generic title would prefer to call themselves according to the country of their ethnic roots.[47] To use the generic title again blurs the distinctive experience of women from different historical roots. Likewise, the evolution of the terms "Indian," "American Indian," and "Native American" tells the story of the dominant white culture's destruction of rich heritages, the disenfranchisement of whole peoples from their lands, as well as the feebleness of attempts to rectify that violence.

These criticisms do not minimize the problems of sexism the women experience within their own cultures. Nor do they minimize the reality of women's subordination in all cultures. They do call the dominant white culture within the women's movement to face its own racism. The challenge is both for accountability and for the creativity to deal with differences. In her closing remarks to the Second Sex Conference, 1979, Audre

Lorde points to a way beyond the usual marginal presence of women of different races and different economic backgrounds at women's conferences:

> It is a particular academic arrogance to assume any discussion of feminist theory in this time and in this place without examining our many differences, and without a significant input from poor women, black and third-world women and lesbians. . . . Advocating the mere tolerance of difference between women is the grossest reformism. It is a total denial of the creative function of difference in our lives. . . .As women, we have been taught to either ignore our differences or to view them as causes for separation and suspicion rather than as forces for change. . . . But community must not mean a shedding of our differences, nor the pathetic pretense that these differences do not exist. . . .If white American feminist theory need not deal with the differences between us, and the resulting differences in aspects of our oppression, then what do you do with the fact that the women who clean your houses and tend your children while you attend conferences on feminist theory are, for the most part, poor and Third World women? What is the theory behind racist feminism? . . .The failure of the academic feminists to recognize difference as a crucial strength is a failure to reach beyond the first patriarchal lesson. Divide and conquer, in our world, must become define and empower.[48]

The growing maturity of the global women's movement presents U.S. women with similar profound challenges. When the U.S. women went to the first World Conference for Women in Mexico City, 1975, they experienced enormous elation and painful confusion. For the most part, the U.S. women who went were unprepared for the anti-U.S. sentiment that pervaded that event. They went desiring to meet women from around the world, to share their common experiences, and to work for women's liberation world-wide.

The meeting in Mexico City proved to be a watershed event. Women did discover their common experiences beyond the cultural, ethnic, religious, ideological, race, and class differences. But they also discovered some profound differences. Many of the women returned home committed to continue to work for the liberation of women, but now on an international scale. Having listened to the problems of women in the so-called Third World countries, they worked to promote "women in development." They created income-generating projects, promoted health, education, and training initiatives, worked for legal and political reform to address women's issues and developed networks with women worldwide for cooperation and coordination. Within the U.S. bureaucracy, they worked to make U.S. AID (Agency for International Development) more aware of women's particular needs in the development process.

However, in 1985, at the close of the International Decade for Women, the DAWN network of Third World women activists, researchers, and policy makers assessed the impact of the Decade: "The studies show that rather than improving, the socioeconomic status of the great majority of Third World women has worsened considerably throughout the Decade. With few exceptions, women's relative access to economic resources, income, and employment has worsened, their burdens of work have increased, and their relative and even absolute health, nutritional, and educational status has declined."[49] The DAWN analysis goes on to challenge the very model of development that had been brought to their countries from the Western countries, often by Western feminists who worked in development.

Ten years of extraordinary efforts in individual and small group projects to move women beyond poverty and dependency had proved inadequate in the face of larger economic, political, and social realities: the debt crisis, world recession, unemployment, war, ecological destruction, unequal and unfair trade practices, the emergence of the global factory system. All these have an impact on women. It has become clear that there can be no sustained promotion of women without a sustainable development within the individual countries; and vice-versa, a truly sustainable economic and political system is not possible without the promotion of women.

The challenge to U.S. feminists is fundamental. What does it mean to be in solidarity with the women of the world? First of all, there is no easy ideology that "Sisterhood is Global."[50] Secondly, feminist analysis of the causes of the oppression of women and its agenda for change must continue to be enlarged and transformed to include all women in all their diversity. Again it is the voices of the women outside the dominant Western culture that point to the future:

> We strongly support the position in this debate that feminism cannot be monolithic in its issues, goals, and strategies, since it constitutes the political expression of the concerns and interests of women from different regions, classes, nationalities, and ethnic backgrounds. While gender subordination has universal elements, feminism cannot be based on a rigid concept of universality that negates the wide variation in women's experience. There is and must be a diversity of feminisms, responsive to the different needs and concerns of different women, and *defined by them for themselves*. This diversity builds on a common opposition to gender oppression and hierarchy, but this is only the first step in articulating and acting upon a political agenda. This heterogeneity gives feminism its dynamism and makes it the most potentially powerful challenge to the status quo [emphasis in original].[51]

The authors continue by pointing out that for some women the problems of nationality, class and race are inextricably linked to their oppression as women. Feminism must be defined to include all these oppressions. But, on the other hand, the struggle to end gender subordination cannot be compromised during the struggle against other oppressions.

For U.S. feminism, this enlarged analysis and agenda cannot help but call into question the role of the U.S. in global politics and economics. Nor can the economic privilege we enjoy as a result of U.S. power be denied. The challenge of global solidarity with women touches not only the subordination of women by men, but also the political and economic subordination of Third World countries by the U.S. There is no easy road to global sisterhood.

Another challenging voice comes from a totally different perspective: Conservative women.[52] These women are deeply committed to the positive role they see themselves playing in the family and in society. They feel that feminism has attacked and undermined what they have known and valued in their roles of mother and wife. They do not consider themselves oppressed by the current structures of the society or in their families. In fact, they are proud of the contributions they make both to stable family life and to stable community life.

They also are deeply troubled by the concept of women's reproductive freedom. Many of them are profoundly anti-abortion. However, not all the women against abortion are anti-feminists. Abortion raises so many deeply troubling questions that it is not a clear litmus test for defining who is a feminist and who is not, although some feminists would make it the defining issue.

Conservative women identify women's primary role as motherhood and see the relationships of men and women as complementary. In this world view, women's responsibility is motherhood and homemaking, and men's responsibility is breadwinning. They do recognize that women can and do pursue other options, but these are viewed more as exceptions rather than the rule.

Many conservative women would hold many of the values that feminists hold, but they would define them as "feminine values." For example, many would be opposed to violence and carry concern for the poor and the disadvantaged. However, their reading of the political and economic reasons for poverty and conflict would differ. Whereas feminists would identify women's poverty within the structural inequalities women experience in the work place, conservatives would identify women's poverty with the breakdown of family life, which is an issue of key importance.

While many conservative women may not be pro-feminist, they are not necessarily anti-feminist. However, within the larger group of conservative women some are anti-feminists. They point to current problems in the society and blame the women's movement. In their view, feminism has caused the stress in family life, failures of marriages, single-heads of households, the feminization of poverty, current divorce laws that leave women in poverty, and the growing need for child care. According to this anti-feminist point of view, all these problems would be alleviated if women left the workforce and returned to their proper roles. Moreover, this political analysis and its agenda is often linked to other very conservative points of view such as pro-capital punishment, anti-communism, strong national defense, reduction of government control, and a return to a less regulated economy.

Conservative women, in fact, are the pillars of the existing social order. As such, they usually have the support and approval of traditional institutions, such as churches and conservative political organizations, especially the new right and many fundamentalist groups. Feminists question how much they are being used by these traditional patriarchal forces. But their voices and their concerns remain and need to be addressed within the larger women's movement.

Finally, there is a large group of women who cannot be defined as feminist, conservative or anti-feminist. They are nonaligned in political terms. They often are critical of the patriarchal structures of the church and society, but they have not found that feminist analyses or rhetoric speaks to their own experience or to their ideas for change. They exist as critics both of traditional structures and attitudes and of the feminist movement. Their most common prefatory remark is "I'm not a feminist, but . . ." Their decision to remain aloof from the movement is a challenge to feminists to understand questions and concerns they are raising and to discover ways to respond to them.

Process Questions

1. What questions do these challenging voices raise for you?
2. What are your questions?

Questions and Contradictions

The women's movement and the feminist theories that continue to shape it are not monolithic, either within the U.S. or globally. There are many issues on which most feminists would agree, but there are also issues where the distinctive ideological roots lead women to take different positions. Several examples will help illustrate how these ideologies influence the positions women and men take.

The question of drafting women is one such example. Liberal feminism would argue, from the point of view of equality, that women as well as men should be called upon to serve their country in the military. Cultural and radical feminism would argue that women, by their nature or because of the values they have developed over the ages, should be opposed to war and refuse to serve in the military. Some would argue that war itself is a patriarchal invention that needs to be challenged by both women and men.

Liberal and cultural feminism would also disagree on the question of protective or special legislation in the work place for women. A recent court case illustrates the differences. In 1982, Lillian Garland lost her job as a receptionist at California Federal Savings and Loan Association after taking time off to have a baby. She appealed her dismissal on the grounds of a California State Law that safeguards a woman's job if she takes up to four months' disability leave for childbirth. Ms. Garland won her initial appeal and returned to her job. However, California Federal Savings and Loan joined by California Chamber of Commerce and the Merchants and Manufacturers Association, a 2900-member employer's group that employs about three million workers, decided to use the case to challenge the California law.

In January 1986, the Supreme Court of the U.S. agreed to hear the case. With almost half of the U.S. labor force now made up of women, and 90% of those expected to have children, the case was critically important for women and the future shape of public policy in relation to maternity/paternity and family. It sparked a widespread and often bitter debate among women's groups.

NOW (National Organization for Women), the ACLU (American Civil Liberties Union), the U.S. Chamber of Commerce, and the Reagan Administration supported California Federal Savings and Loan in seeking to declare the law unconstitutional. This unusual coalition, bound only by a similar liberal perspective that separates public and private responsibility, argued that the law gives special treatment to women and therefore discriminates against men. In addition, women's groups feared that such a law would lead to further discrimination against women, because they will be seen as a potential financial liability to a company.

Following an argument shaped by cultural feminism, Marian Johnston, the lawyer defending the California law, argued that it is not a question of special rights for pregnant women but of a law to correct an "imbalance caused by the biological fact that only women have babies."[53] She further argued that current disability leave (pregnancy is considered a legal disability under the Federal Pregnancy Discrimination Act) is not adequate to cover the kinds of disability that childbearing may cause. Furthermore, because the U.S. has no public policy on maternity/paternity leave, it is not available everywhere but depends upon company and workplace policy. The Supreme Court upheld the California law.

On the issue of legal pornography, radical feminism splits with liberal feminism. This issue was brought to a vote in the Minneapolis City Council. Radical feminists worked to have pornography outlawed on the grounds that it provoked men to act violently toward women. Liberal feminism as well as the larger liberal community argued that such a law would be contrary to freedom of expression as guaranteed by the Constitution. The radical feminist position won in City Council vote, but the mayor refused to sign the proposal into law because he believed it was unconstitutional.

Differences also begin to surface when feminists begin addressing the questions of economic development and economic independence for women. Liberal feminism advocates moving women ahead within the present economic structures; socialist feminism calls for a transformation of those economic structures for the purpose of more just distribution of power and resources.

Process Questions

1. These examples are only illustrative of the many new challenges and public policy questions the women's movement is bringing to our social structures.

2. What are some other issues that confront us as a church and society?

If feminism is to be a transforming power in our world, the ideologies that shape it need to be understood, both for the contributions they bring to our analysis of women's experience and for the problems they carry as we seek a more just world. The purpose of all analysis is to enable us to identify how the key structures of our world function: political structures, economic structures, sociological structures and cultural structures. Feminist analysis reveals how deeply patriarchy shapes all these structures.

Analysis, however, is a descriptive tool. It enables us to recognize the social structures of our world. It does not prescribe solutions or courses of action to address those structures if they are unjust. Often what appears to be the most obvious solution to correct an unjust situation in the short run does not necessarily hold promise for a truly transformed world for all— women, men, the young, the old, the unborn, people of all races, people from the nations of the Southern hemisphere, the differently-abled. And as we have noted, feminists, shaped by different ideological perspectives, do not all agree on the directions to move. For the task of social transformation we must move from analysis to social ethics.

Within the Catholic tradition, social ethics has been evolving through a body of social teaching that has received extensive development within the last 100 years. However, Catholic social thought is limited by its patriarchal bias. Before it can offer a meaningful ethical perspective to bring to the dialogue for more just social structures, Catholic social thought itself needs a feminist revision. In the next chapter, I will begin to address that task.

Endnotes

1. Adrienne Rich, *The Dream of a Common Language,* "Twenty-one Love Poems: XIII" (New York: W.W. Norton and Company, Inc., 1978), p. 31.

2. See Joe Holland and Peter Henriot, SJ, *Social Analysis: Linking Faith and Justice,* Revised and Enlarged Edition (Maryknoll, NY: Orbis Books, 1985) for a more detailed introduction to social analysis within the justice context.

3. Myra Marx Ferree and Beth B. Hess, *Controversy and Coalition: The New Feminist Movement* (Boston: Twayne Publishers, 1985), p. 64; Jo Freeman, *The Politics of Women's Liberation* (New York: David McKay Company, Inc., 1975), p. 118ff.; and Barbara Sinclair Deckard, *The Women's Movement: Political, Socioeconomic and Psychological Issues,* 3rd edition (New York: Harper Row, Publishers, Inc., 1983), p. 330.

4. Feminist consciousness-raising is not unlike Paulo Freire's theory of liberating education as described in his book, *The Pedagogy of the Oppressed* (New York: Herder and Herder, 1970). See also Anne Hope and Sally Timmel, *Training for Transformation: A Handbook for Community Workers,* 3 Vols. (Gweru, Zimbabwe: Mambo Press, 1984) for a practical implementation of the Freire method of liberating education. *Training for Transformation* is available through Center of Concern, Washington, DC.

5. Marilyn French, *Beyond Power: On Women, Men, and Morals* (New York: Summit Books, 1985), p. 442.

6. Heidi Hartmann, "The Unhappy Marriage of Marxism and Feminism: Towards a More Progressive Union," in *Women and Revolution,* ed. by Lydia Sargent (Boston: South End Press, 1981), p. 13.

7. Nancy Hartsock, "Fundamental Feminism: Process and Perspective," in *Building Feminist Theory,* (New York: Longman, 1981), p. 36. This theory of connection between personal transformation and social transformation relates to the theory of praxis as defined by Paulo Freire. See *The Pedagogy of the Oppressed.*

8. Hartsock, p. 36.

9. The text used is as quoted in Henry F. Graff, *America: The Glorious Republic* (Boston: Houghton Mifflin Company, 1985), p. 816. Punctuation and capitalization follows accepted sources.

10. *The Feminist Papers,* ed. by Alice Rossi (New York: Bantam Books, 1974), p. 416. See also Chapter 2, p. 16 of this work.

11. For a more extensive treatment of these ideas see Carol Gilligan, *In A Different Voice* (Cambridge, Massachusetts: Harvard University Press, 1983) and Robert N. Bellah, et al., *Habits of the Heart* (New York: Harper and Row, Publishers, 1986).

12. Alison M. Jaggar, *Feminist Politics And Human Nature* (Totowa, New Jersey: Rowman and Allanheld, 1983), p. 47.

13. In the context, the word "culture" is not used in the anthropological meaning of the value context of a society.

14. See Chapter 2, pp. 17-18.

15. Josephine Donovan, *Feminist Theory: The Intellectual Traditions Of American Feminism* (New York: Frederick Ungar Publishing Co., 1985), p. 32.

16. Donovan, pp. 31-32.

17. Olive Banks, *Faces of Feminism* (Oxford, UK: Basil Blackwell Ltd., 1981), p. 63.

18. For a more extensive history of these efforts, see Banks, pp. 63-117.

19. See note 11.

20. Donovan, p. 62.

21. Jaggar, p. 83-84; and Donovan, p. 141-142.

22. Because of this emphasis on women's culture, some theorists use the name cultural feminism for radical feminism. While both cultural and radical feminism find some common ground in their approach to women's culture, they arise out of very different historical roots.

23. N.Y. Radical Feminists, "Politics of Ego," in *Radical Feminism,* edited by Anne Koedt, Ellen Levine, and Anita Rapone (New York: Quadrangle Books, 1973), p. 379. First published in *Notes From The Second Year.*

24. Shulamith Firestone, *The Dialectic Of Sex: The Case For Feminist Revolution* (New York: Bantam Books, Inc., 1971), p. 1.

25. Adrienne Rich, "Compulsory Heterosexuality and Lesbian Existence," *Signs: Journal of Women in Culture And Society,* V:4 (Summer, 1980), pp. 631-60.

26. See pp. 13-14 in Chapter 2.

27. The term "post-marxian" indicates that socialist feminism draws upon the categories of marxist analysis but enlarges them with contemporary insights. As such, it should not be interpreted as primarily seeking to advance the marxist agenda but as seeking to develop a theoretical framework and political agenda that will lead to women's liberation, particularly in relation to the structures of advanced liberal capitalism as we live it today. The analysis of the relationship between marxism and socialist feminism remains a lively debate among marxists, feminists and political theorists. See for example, Lydia Sargent, ed., *Women And Revolution;* Allison Jaggar, *Feminist Politics And Human Nature,* especially the chapters "Traditional Marxism and Human Nature," "Socialist Feminism and Human Nature," "The Politics of Traditional Marxism," "The Politics of Socialist Feminism," and "Feminist Politics and Epistemology: Justifying Feminist Theory." See also Maxine Molyneux, "Mobilization Without Emancipation? Women's Interests, State and Revolution," in *Transition and Development: Problems of Third World Socialism,* eds. Richard R. Fagen, Carmen Diana Deere, and Jose Luis Coraggio (New York: Monthly Review Press, Center for the Study of the Americas, 1986); and *Building Feminist Theory: Essays From Quest* (New York: Longman, 1981).

28. Ferree and Hess, p. 154.

29. Jaggar, p. 130.

30. Hartmann, p. 12; and Firestone.

31. Hartmann, p. 15.

32. Hartmann, p. 22.

33. Jaggar, p. 320.

34. Jaggar, p. 318.

35. Rosalind Petchesky, "Reproductive Freedom: Beyond 'A Woman's Right to Choose,'" *Signs: Journal Of Women In Culture And Society,* 5:4 (Summer, 1980) p. 683. See also, Jaggar, pp. 318ff.

36. Jaggar, p. 320.

37. Hilda Scott, *Does Socialism Liberate Women?* (Boston: Beacon Press, 1974), p. 190.

38. Bell Hooks, *Ain't I A Woman: Black Women And Feminism* (Boston: South End Press, 1981), p. 125.

39. For a detailed history of racism in the women's movement, see Angela Y. Davis, *Women Race and Class* (New York: Random House, 1981); and Hooks.

40. See *This Bridge Called My Back: Writings By Radical Women Of Color,* 2nd edition, eds. Cherrie Moraga and Gloria Anzaldua (New York: Kitchen Table: Women of Color Press, 1983) and Letty Cottin Pogrebin, "Anti-Semitism in the Women's Movement," MS (June, 1982).

41. As quoted in *But Some Of Us Are Brave: Black Women's Studies,* ed. by Gloria T. Hull, Patricia Bell Scott, and Barbara Smith (New York: The Feminist Press, 1982), p. 49.

42. Hooks, p. 122.

43. Hooks, p 123.

44. A Louis Harris Virginia Slims poll conducted in 1972 revealed that 62% of black women polled as compared to 45% of while women polled supported efforts to change woman's status in society. 65% of the black women polled as compared to 35% of the white women polled were sympathetic to women's liberation groups. As quoted in Hooks, p. 148. More recently, a *Newsweek* survey in 1986 found that 65% of the black women polled identified themselves as feminist as compared to 56% of the white women polled. As quoted in *Decade Of Achievement 1977-1987,* A Report of The National Women's Conference Center, ed. Susanna Downie et al. (Beaver Dam, WI: National Women's Conference Center, 1988), p.1.

45. Hooks, p. 139.

46. See note #41.

47. Ada Maria Isasi-Diaz and Yolanda Tarango, *Hispanic Women: Prophetic Voice In The Church* (San Francisco: Harper and Row, 1988), p. x.

48. Audre Lorde, "The Master's Tools Will Never Dismantle The Master's House," as printed in *This Bridge Called My Back: Writings Of Radical Women Of Color,* pp. 98-100.

49. Gita Sen and Caren Grown, *Development, Crises, And Alternative Visions: Third World Women's Perspectives* (New York: Monthly Review Press, 1987), p. 16.

50. Robin Morgan, ed., *Sisterhood Is Global* (Garden City, NY: Anchor Books, 1984).

51. Sen and Grown, p. 19.

52. I am using the word "conservative" here in its classic meaning of conserving the good we have known.

53. *New York Times* (February 2, 1986), p. 1.

4

A Sign of Our Times

The People of God believe that
it is led by the Spirit of God . . . .
Motivated by this faith, it labors to decipher
authentic signs of God's presence and purpose in
the happenings, needs, and desires of our age.
                                    —*Gaudium Et Spes*[1]

A central thesis shaping this book is the recognition that the women's movement is creating one of the most far-reaching social revolutions of our time. The very process of women redefining their self-understanding and seeking mutual and equal relationships with men in all dimensions of life is creating new realities and different social needs in our lives. It is shaping and reshaping our expectations and experiences in personal relationships and in all our social and ecclesial institutions. Moreover, these realities and needs are making new claims on traditional social systems and structures—governments, schools, families, churches, synagogues, social services, businesses.[2] They have also opened new horizons for social ethics as the profound but subtle shifting of social institutions has become evident and we are discovering that the women's movement is not only about justice for women. It is about the future shape of our church and our world.

On these horizons of the future, feminism and Catholic social thought meet in the search for a more just and transformed world. In the search for that future, I believe a dialogue between feminist social theory and Catholic social thought would be fruitful for both.

The dialogue is necessary to correct the patriarchy embedded in Catholic social thought. It can be identified as patriarchal for several reasons: 1) it was written by men, primarily about men; 2) its bias is androcentric, that is, it assumes that man, in this case, white Western man, is normative for the human; and 3) when women are included, they are defined from a patriarchal point of view.

Given this patriarchal bias, how useful is such a dialogue for Catholic feminists? The same question exists for liberal feminists and socialist feminists. Liberal feminism is a feminist revision of the liberal doctrine articulated by men for white, land-owning males of the eighteenth century. Socialist feminism is a feminist revision of marxist thought, also written by men whose analysis was shaped by the male experience. In the process of these revisions, both liberal feminism and socialist feminism have expanded the boundaries of liberal and marxist thought while enriching feminist thought. A feminist revision of Catholic social thought will similarly expand the horizons of that tradition as well as give Catholic feminists a perspective from which to engage in dialogue with the various ideologies of feminism—liberal, cultural, radical, and socialist—as we participate in the social revolution being shaped by the women's movement. It could also prove to be a strong ally in women's liberation struggle.

In this chapter, I will give a brief overview of Catholic social thought, review historically how women have been treated in that tradition, offer an initial feminist revision of that tradition, and sketch the outlines of a dialogue between a feminist-revised Catholic social theory and the various feminist ideologies. In the process, I continue to invite the readers to engage in this dialogue as we together seek the kind of transformation that holds promise for true liberation for women and men in both the church and the society.

Catholic Social Thought

In this context, the term "Catholic social thought" is used to cover that body of papal and church teaching which begins with Pope Leo XIII's social encyclical *Rerum Novarum (The Condition Of Labor)*, in 1891, and extends to official church documents which address social issues today. A listing of these documents would include *Quadragesimo Anno (The Reconstruction Of The Social Order)*, 1931; *Mater Et Magistra (Christianity And Social Progress)*, 1961; *Pacem In Terris (Peace On Earth)*, 1963; *Gaudium Et Spes (The Church In The Modern World)*, 1965; *Populorum Progressio (The Progress Of Peoples)*, 1967; *Medellin Documents,* 1968; *Octogesima Adveniens (A Call To Action)*, 1971; *Justice In The World,* 1971; *The Puebla Document,* 1979; *Laborem Exercens (On Human Labor)*, 1981; *The Challenge Of Peace,* 1983; *Economic Justice For All,* 1986; and *Sollicitudo Rei Socialis (The Social Concerns Of The*

Church), 1988.[4] It is a rich heritage of teaching on the meaning of the human person in society. It is also an evolving tradition, responding to the historical situations in which the church finds itself.

A study of church documents that articulate Catholic social ethics from *Rerum Novarum* (*On The Condition Of The Working Class*), 1891, to *Sollicitudo Rei Socialis* (*On The Social Concerns Of The Church*), 1988, reveals a dramatic evolution in attitude and methodology.[5] This evolution follows the emerging human consciousness of personal dignity, freedom, and equality that has characterized the 20th century, as well as the recognition that a narrow application of the so-called objective principles of natural law is insufficient to respond to the historical and subjective complexities of human persons interacting in the social order.

Vatican Council II stands as a watershed moment in the evolution of Catholic social thought. During this historic Council, the church shifted from a defensive stance of isolation from the trends of the contemporary world to a recognition that the church must be an actor in shaping that world. The shift was not only for the institution of the church, but also for the members of the church. In imaging the church as the People of God, the Council called upon the whole church to become active participants in shaping the social order. Religious conviction and action were no longer confined to the private sphere of peoples' lives; they were also to shape their political, social, and economic lives.

Finally, the influence of liberation theology is struggling to take hold in the methodology of Catholic social thought. With its insistence on the primacy of the historical context as well as its insistence on the necessity of praxis, liberation theology is enhancing Catholic social ethics by addressing not only the causes of social injustice but the process of liberation itself. That process begins with individual people reflecting on their experience and moving to analysis and theological reflection on that experience as the basis for their pastoral action—praxis. It is in the praxis that Catholic social theory and the church's social mission meet. The recent U. S. bishops' pastorals on peace, on the U.S. economy, and on women's concerns partially introduce this methodology into the shaping of church teaching.

An extensive analysis of this body of teaching is beyond either the scope or the intent of this book. I simply want to identify some of the major themes that have shaped Catholic social thought and bring these themes into dialogue with the various feminist ideologies. The following 12 themes are generally identified as central to Catholic social teaching on the meaning and relationships of human persons in society.

1. Link of religious and social dimensions of life. The "social"—the human construction of the world—is not "secular" in the sense of being outside of God's plan, but is intimately involved with the dynamic of the Reign of God. Therefore, faith and justice are necessarily linked together.

2. Dignity of the human person. Made in the image of God, women and men have a preeminent place in the social order. Human dignity can be recognized and protected only in community with others. The fundamental question to ask about social development is: What is happening to people?

3. Political and economic rights. All human persons enjoy inalienable rights, which are political-legal (e.g., voting, free speech, migration) and social-economic (e.g., food, shelter, work, education). These are realized in community. Essential for the promotion of justice and solidarity, these rights are to be respected and protected by all the institutions of society.

4. Option for the poor. A preferential love should be shown to the poor, whose needs and rights are given special attention in God's eyes. "Poor" is understood to refer to the economically disadvantaged who, as a consequence of their status, suffer oppression and powerlessness.

5. Link of love and justice. Love of neighbor is an absolute demand for justice, because charity must manifest itself in actions and structures which respect human dignity, protect human rights, and facilitate human development. To promote justice is to transform structures which block love.

6. Promotion of the common good. The common good is the sum total of all those conditions of social living—economic, political, cultural—which make it possible for women and men readily and fully to achieve the perfection of their humanity. Individual rights are always experienced within the context of promotion of the common good. There is also an international common good.

7. Subsidiarity. Responsibilities and decisions should be attended to as closely as possible to the level of individual initiative in local communities and institutions. Mediating structures of families, neighborhoods, community groups, small businesses, and local governments should be fostered and participated in. But larger government structures do have a role when greater social coordination and regulation are necessary for the common good.

8. Political participation. Democratic participation in decision-making is the best way to respect the dignity and liberty of people. The government is the instrument by which people cooperate together in order to achieve the common good. The international common good requires participation in international organizations.

9. Economic Justice. The economy is for the people, and the resources of the earth are to be shared equitably by all. Human work is the key to contemporary social questions. Labor takes precedence over both capital and technology in the production process. Just wages and the right of workers to organize are to be respected.

10. Stewardship. All property has a "social mortgage." People are to respect and share the resources of the earth, since we are all part of the community of creation. By our work, we are co-creators in the continuing development of the earth.

11. Global solidarity. We belong to one human family and as such have mutual obligations to promote the rights and development of all people across the world, irrespective of national boundaries. In particular, the rich nations have responsibilities toward the poor nations, and the structures of the international order must reflect justice.

12. Promotion of peace. Peace is the fruit of justice and is dependent upon right order among humans and among nations. The arms race must cease and progressive disarmament take place if the future is to be secure. In order to promote peace and the conditions of peace, an effective international authority is necessary.[6]

Process Questions

1. How have you been shaped by these principle themes?
2. What questions do you have regarding these themes?
3. Is there any theme you would add? Any you would remove? Why?

Catholic social thought claims that these themes apply universally to all human persons. It is at this juncture that a feminist analysis needs to unmask the patriarchal bias that historically has shaped the evolution of Catholic social ethics. In developing a feminist analysis of Catholic social thought, two questions need to be addressed: How does Catholic social thought deal with women? Does it accurately reflect women's experience?

Women in Catholic Social Thought

Before the encyclicals of Pope John XXIII, women are seldom mentioned in social documents except implicitly under generic statements regarding the dignity of "man" (that is, the human person), and under the category of "family." In the first social encyclical, Leo XIII's *Rerum Novarum* (*On The Condition Of Labor*), 1891, women are implicitly included under the concern for the family. Leo XIII's world view was authoritarian and paternalistic, with clearly defined roles for everyone.[7] For Leo XIII, women's place and role was clear, divinely ordained, and therefore, in no need of elaboration. It was the worker and the family that occupied his concern. Workers were understood as men. Justice for workers meant that the rights of their families would be protected and that they, as heads of families, would receive just wages. Women as wives and mothers would be economically dependent on this just wage of the working father. This particular point of view continues to shape Catholic social teaching up to the present.

In *Quadragesimo Anno* (*The Reconstruction Of The Social Order*), by Pius XI, 1931, women do specifically appear as workers. They are mentioned in the section "Support of the Worker and His [sic] Family." Women and children are mentioned in the same sentence: "But to abuse the years of childhood and the limited strength of women is grossly wrong."[8] Both are considered dependent and in need of special protection. Women are not seen as autonomous adults. This habit of identifying women with children and other dependent persons has been the accepted norm in most Catholic writing, particularly in canon law.[9]

The first time women enter Catholic social thought in their own right is in John XXIII's encyclical *Pacem In Terris* (*Peace On Earth*), 1963. He identifies three "distinctive characteristics" of our age—signs of our times: the rise of the working class, the participation of women in public life, and the emergence of new nations.[10] John writes: "Secondly, it is obvious to everyone that women are now taking a part in public life. This is happening more rapidly perhaps in nations with a Christian tradition, and more slowly, but broadly, among peoples who have inherited other traditions or cultures. Since women are becoming ever more conscious of their human dignity, they will not tolerate being treated as inanimate objects or mere instruments, but claim, both in domestic and in public life, the rights and duties that befit a human person."[11]

Moreover, in this encyclical John declares that every person is endowed with intelligence and free will and has universal and inviolable rights and duties. He identifies these rights as political, economic, social, cultural, and moral. By including women specifically in this document, he is explicitly declaring that women have the same rights and duties as men.

With the writings of John XXIII and the opening of the Second Vatican Council in 1962, the world view of Catholic social thought had altered significantly. The static, hierarchical, authoritarian, and paternalistic world of Leo XIII had shifted to a view shaped by historical consciousness, a recognition of the radical freedom of the human person, and the autonomy of the world from religion's control.

Gaudium Et Spes (*The Pastoral Constitution On The Church In The Modern World*) was the centerpiece of social teaching that emerged from Vatican Council II. The document rings with affirmation of the fundamental dignity of the human person. Because the document uses the Latin word *homo*—the human person—rather than *vir*—the male person—its references to the human person, humanity, and the entire human family clearly intended to include women in this fundamental human dignity. Moreover, it states that "with respect to the fundamental rights of the person, every type of discrimination, whether social or cultural, whether based on sex, race, color, social condition, language, or religion, is to be overcome and eradicated as contrary to God's intent."[12] However, at times the language of the document slips and seems to reveal that the Fathers of the

Council are really talking about men. Such words as "brotherly dialogue" and "brotherhood" exclude women.[13]

It is interesting to note that women appear in their own right for the first time in relation to a perceived problem. The first such reference comes in a section on "Imbalances in the Modern World": "As for the family, discord results from demographic, economic, and social pressures, or from difficulties which arise between succeeding generations, or from new social relationships between men and women."[14] Setting the "new social relationships" under the heading "Imbalances in the Modern World" reflects a patriarchal interpretation of the changes related to women's rising consciousness.

In the section on the "Dignity of the Human Person," the document reads, "But God did not create man [*homo*] as a solitary. For from the beginning 'male and female he created them' " (Gen. 1:27) [Brackets mine]. The discussion of marriage and family succeeds in talking about women and men, spouses and parents even-handedly.

However, in the section on culture, the traditional ambiguity concerning women's rights appears. Recognizing that humans are the authors of culture the document states, "In every group or nation, there is an ever-increasing number of men and women who are conscious that they themselves are the artisans and the authors of the culture of their community." Several sections beyond this statement of mutual responsibility and participation, the document qualifies itself: "Women are now employed in almost every area of life. It is appropriate that they should be able to assume their full *proper role in accordance with their own nature.* Everyone should acknowledge and favor the proper and necessary participation of women in cultural life"[15] [emphasis mine]. We are confronted here with a statement that women's nature, and therefore presumably their rights contingent upon that nature, are different from men's nature and rights. We are confronted with a concept of a dual human nature—there is human nature, which is equated with men's nature, and then there is women's nature.

Women as women next appear in Paul VI's *Octogesima Adveniens* (*A Call To Action*), 1971. He continues the concept of a dual human nature:

> Similarly, in many countries a charter for women which would put an end to an actual discrimination and would establish relationships of equality in rights and of respect for their dignity

is the object of study and at times of lively demands. We do not have in mind that false equality which would deny the distinctions laid down by the Creator himself and which would be in contradiction with woman's *proper role*, which is of such capital importance, at the heart of the family as well as within society. Development in legislation should on the contrary be directed to protecting her *proper vocation* and at the same time recognizing her independence as a person, and her equal rights to participate in cultural, economic, social and political life[16] [emphasis mine].

Can a person having a proper role and vocation, pre-determined by her nature and needing special protection, still be independent and have equal rights with a person who has no such qualifying and limiting definitions pre-determined by his nature?

Justice In The World, the statement of the 1971 Synod of Bishops introduces the question of justice in the church regarding women. The document declares that anyone who ventures to preach justice must first be perceived as being just. It then lists specific rights that must be preserved within the church, namely, all ordinary rights, a decent wage, security, promotion, freedom of thought and expression, proper judicial procedures, and participation in decision-making. In particular, the document states that women have equal rights and responsibilities without any qualification: "We also urge that women should have their own share of responsibility and participation in the community life of society and likewise of the church."[17]

Justice In The World also speaks of the social movements among peoples as "a new awareness which shakes them out of any fatalistic resignation and which spurs them on to liberate themselves and to be responsible for their own destiny."[18] Furthermore, it introduces the need to change social structures if justice is to become a reality in people's lives: "This desire [for human rights], however, will not satisfy the expectations of our time if it ignores the objective obstacles which social structures place in the way of conversion of hearts, or even of the realization of ideal charity."[19]

This document brings together several powerful themes that support women's struggle for justice in the church and in the world. In calling for justice in the church, especially for women, and in affirming social movements whereby people assume responsibility for their own lives to change oppressive structures, *Justice In The World* affirms women's struggle for liberation.

In *Laborem Exercens* (*On Human Labor*), 1981, John Paul II makes explicit his views on the proper role and vocation of women. The encyclical, while recognizing that women do work outside the home, continues the tradition that the primary role of women is to be responsible for the family and the primary role of men is to be responsible for economic support of the family. John Paul continues the position that the man, as head of the family, is entitled to a family wage. In reality, he is re-asserting the patriarchal model of the family. He calls for a "social re-evaluation of the mother's role," calling for a society to support a woman in this role, not inhibiting her freedom or in any other way penalizing her as compared with other women. He speaks of women "having to abandon" their tasks as mothers as being wrong from the point of view of society and the family. Finally, he insists that "true advancement of women requires that labor should be structured in such a way that women do not have to pay for their advancement by abandoning what is specific to them and at the expense of the family, in which women as mothers have an irreplaceable role."[20]

John Paul does not call for a concomitant social re-evaluation of fatherhood.

Two church documents introduce gender into their analysis of the contemporary world: The *Puebla Document* published after the meeting of the Latin American bishops in Puebla, Mexico, 1979 and the U.S bishops' pastoral on the economy, *Economic Justice For All: Catholic Social Teaching And The U.S. Economy, 1986.*

The *Puebla Document* identifies the marginalization of women from political, economic and social life as the result of "cultural atavisms—male predominance, unequal wages, deficient education, etc."[21] It further identifies some specifics of that marginalization: prostitution as a result of stifling economic situation, exploitation of women in the work place, the overburdening of women in the family, and the church's undervaluing of women. The document speaks of being encouraged by women's initiatives and growing consciousness.[22]

The document also calls the church to "consider" the equality and dignity of women and recognize the mission of women in the church and in the world. It recognizes women's aspirations for liberation as an "authentic sign of the times," while specifically underlining "the fundamental role of the woman as mother, the defender of life and the home educator."[23] This document marks a significant advance in Catholic social teaching's recognition of the complex reality that shapes women's lives.

The U.S. bishops' pastoral on the economy, *Economic Justice For All: Catholic Social Teaching And The U.S. Economy,* treats the complexity of the economic issues faced by women with some depth. Women's economic issues are treated integrally throughout the whole document rather than in just one section, thereby avoiding the implicit statement that these are only "women's issues" rather than problems of the economic system. For the first time in a church document, the language is clearly gender-specific in order to illumine the different economic issues faced by women and men. The causes of the "feminization of poverty" are examined and condemned. The document calls for greater economic justice for women in the work place, and it recognizes the changing patterns in family life with mutual responsibilities for both fathers and mothers.

The various drafts of the pastoral addressed the mutual responsibilities of both parents in family life, but for the first time, in the final document, the position of John Paul II emphasizing the special role of mothers in the families was introduced: "We affirm the principle enunciated by John Paul II that society's institutions and policies should be structured so that mothers of young children are not forced by economic necessity to leave their children for jobs outside the home."[24] The church teaching continues to be caught on the horns of the dilemma of its dual anthropology: it insists women have full and equal human rights and responsibilities—politically, economically, socially, culturally, and ecclesially—as befits a human person. However, in continuing to insist upon women's proper nature and role as something distinct from human nature, it restricts women's potential for realizing these rights.

The purpose of raising these issues is not to deny or denigrate the social role and value of women who choose childrearing and homemaking as their primary work. Rather it is to bring into perspective the multiple roles and potential of women. Furthermore, to so emphasize that women are primarily responsible for the quality of family life diminishes the social role and value of fatherhood. It disenfranchises men from the full potential of their fatherhood while it disenfranchises women from the full potential of their personhood. Until the church is able to recognize the mutuality of women and men in all dimensions of life, its reflection and teaching will remain inadequate to contemporary realities.

Sollicitudo Rei Socialis (The Social Concern Of The Church), 1988, John Paul II's encyclical on international development, was written to celebrate the 20th anniversary of Paul VI's *Populorum Progressio (On The Progress Of Peoples)*. Both these documents lack a gender perspective; women are included under the generic terms of "man," "humanity," "human family." In several instances, John Paul II does name women as women, specifically when he is outlining the failure of the development process. For example, "Looking at all the various sectors—the production and distribution of foodstuffs, hygiene, health and housing, availability of drinking water, working conditions (especially for women), life expectancy and other economic and social indicators . . . ."[25] It is worth noting that in the section on demography, John Paul II develops his argument about population and the birthrate without once mentioning women. The encyclical does not add any new insights concerning women to Catholic social thought. Nor does it contain any of the insights of current feminist critiques of the development processes.

Process Questions

1. What do you think are the most significant issues about the way Catholic social thought addresses the question of women?

2. What do you think Catholic social thought lacks in its outlook on women?

Toward a Feminist
Revision of Catholic Social Thought

Before critiquing some of the central themes in Catholic social thought from a feminist perspective, the issue of methodology needs to be raised.

How is Catholic social thought developed and who participates in its development? All Catholic teaching is shaped by reflections on the "Word of God in the scriptures, on tradition, on the teaching of the church, on the signs of the times, and on the eschatological pull of the future."[26] Having recognized this reality, it is also necessary to recognize that all these resources are in the process of a feminist revisioning because they all are shaped by a patriarchal bias. However, in this book, I will speak only to the issue of "reading the signs of the times." The decision to focus on this method is two-fold: 1) identifying the "signs of the times" is particularly germane in Catholic social thought and in the church's social mission; and 2) revealing the patriarchal bias in one method points to its presence in other methods.

In *Pacem In Terris*, John XXIII introduced the reading of the "signs of the times" into the methodology of developing Catholic social thought. He was drawing upon the "basic Christian belief that God continues to speak in and through human history":

> The Church looks to the world and discovers there God's presence. Signs both reveal God's presence in the world and manifest God's designs for the world. Implicit in this truth is that theology must go beyond the purely deductive and speculative. History ceases to be the mere context for the application of binding principles, which are derived uniquely from speculative and philosophical reasoning. It becomes the place of on-going revelation.[27]

The rise of women's consciousness of their own dignity is a "sign of our times." As such it demands the attention of the church. The church cannot simply reach back into its tradition to address this reality because it "lacks a strong tradition regarding the equality and basic dignity and worth of women."[28] Furthermore, the current reflection and articulation of women's experience is raising new issues both in the society and in the church.

Feminists rightly raise the question, "Who reads the 'signs of the times'?" Or even more pointedly, "Whose reading is listened to?" The further question then becomes, "Who decides on the response to these 'signs' in framing the social mission of the church?" Catholic social teaching has been the province of the patriarchal church: men are the sole authors, only men sit in a decision-making capacity in the deliberative bodies of the church—ecumenical councils, synods, conferences of bishops. When women are present, at most they have a consultative role to play.

If women's rising consciousness is a manifestation of God's design for the world, as both John XXIII in *Pacem In Terris* and the *Puebla Docu-*

ment declare, can Catholic teaching continue to be authentic if the voices of women are kept silent and/or circumscribed by men's interpretation? I am reminded of Gamaliel's intervention to the Sanhedrin in the early days of the founding of the church: "If this enterprise, this movement of theirs, is of human origin it will break up of its own accord; but if it does in fact come from God you will not only be unable to destroy them, but you might find yourselves fighting against God" (Acts 5:38-40).

For Catholic feminists, this sense of the "rightness" of their struggle for liberation is shaped by an understanding of their quest as a "sign of our time." This quest is not a struggle for self-aggrandizement as its critics accuse, but a quest for the integrity of the gospel and the authenticity of the church in the contemporary world. It is also a struggle for the liberation of our concept of God from the limiting images and perspective that only male images of the divine can bring.

Finally, if the dialogue between feminism and the church—the People of God and its institutional organization—could open up to mutuality and co-responsibility in the shaping of its teaching and the framing of its mission, a more authentic reading of God's design for the world would begin to reveal itself: a design less hampered or distorted by arrogance and egoism among either the men or the women of the church.

The key for a feminist revision of Catholic social thought is to re-define the dual-nature concept that shapes the church's thinking about the dignity of the human person. In seeking to recognize that women and men are different, it has created the dilemma of human nature—read "man's nature"—and woman's "proper" nature. Feminism rejects this duality, pointing out that the very concept of woman's "proper" nature has been used to keep women in a subordinate position in all social structures. In framing a theological anthropology on the meaning of the human, feminism insists on the foundational category of personhood, not on proper roles. Sex is a secondary category.

When this dual-nature concept is revised, several other themes of Catholic social thought are immediately opened for a revised analysis. Among them I would list political and economic rights, political participation, economic justice, preferential option for the poor, the common good, and subsidiarity.

Political and Economic rights. While, theoretically, Catholic social thought agrees that there is only one human nature, practically, in shaping its application of human rights and duties, it uses a dual nature and role approach. For example, within the tradition, economic rights of workers are primarily presented as men's economic rights. The right to a family wage as articulated from Leo XIII in *Rerum Novarum* to John Paul II in *Laborem Exercens* is understood as a wage paid to the father as head of the family to ensure that there is sufficient income for the mother to stay at home to perform her "primary" responsibilities.

Catholic social thought remains ambiguous on the question of women's economic rights. It would probably be more accurate to say that given its patriarchal bias, it has never thought through the implications of economic rights in relation to women. However, unless women have economic rights in their own right, they will remain economically dependent either upon their husbands, fathers or other male members of the family, or they will become dependent upon the welfare state.

Economic independence is one of the keys to women's liberation. When women and men both enjoy equal economic rights and opportunities, their relationships in all other dimensions of life, such as homemaking and childrearing, can indeed move toward mutuality. The concept of the "family wage," rooted in the patriarchal model of family, needs to be re-defined as economic codependence within an egalitarian model of family.

Furthermore, this concept of the father as the primary breadwinner in the family continues to justify treating women and men differently in the work place. A woman's participation in the work force is considered secondary for two reasons; 1) her primary work is defined as homemaking and childrearing; and 2) her income from her job outside the home is considered secondary or even superfluous for the economic well-being of the family. Therefore, women justifiably can be paid less and have fewer opportunities for advancement. Not only is this reasoning untrue to a growing number of women and families, it also puts women at a disadvantage in both the home and the work place. The clearest example we have of this disadvantage is the current phenomenon in the U.S. called the "feminization of poverty."[29] The phenomenon should be more accurately described as the "pauperization of women and children." As long as we do not positively think in terms of women's economic rights, as a society we will continue to have structures that enforce economic dependency on most women. In speaking of an option for the poor, the majority of whom are women and children, Catholic social thought needs to be more explicit in applying the principle of economic rights to women.

The same kind of disadvantage emerges when the question of political rights and political participation is discussed. Theoretically, Catholic social thought would argue for women's inalienable right as a human person to political participation at all levels. However, practically, by insisting that women's "proper role" is motherhood and by defining that role as including the primary responsibility for childrearing, the church limits women's participation in political processes. A full recognition of women's inalienable right to participation in social structures demands a change in the church's perspective on women's "proper nature and role." Such a change would also force the church to recognize and correct its own denial of women's right to participate in orders and decision-making within its own institutional structures.

Both feminism and Catholic social thought recognize in their analyses the centrality of the question of women as childbearers. But their responses differ radically. Catholic social teaching takes a protective and limiting approach to women as a result of this reality. Women's potential and nature are circumscribed by one reality, the fact that they bear children. The nature of woman is defined by one function that some/most women experience. The nature of man is never defined according to his narrow function as father.

Feminism asserts, on the other hand, that women should not be defined or circumscribed by this single reality. Furthermore, feminism insists that because women alone carry the responsibility for childbearing and, in most cases, for childrearing, only women should have control over this question. Socialist feminism enlarges the discussion of reproductive choice to include the responsibility of society to provide adequate support for the well-being of mothers and children: adequate nutrition, housing, health care, child care, education and a safe environment. It moves the question beyond the biological reality and includes the common good in order to avoid the individualism of the current liberal and radical position that it is solely a woman's "right to choose."

In speaking of reproductive freedom, the distinction needs to be made between a woman controlling her fertility through birth control methods and a woman choosing to have an abortion. Among feminists, there is universal agreement that women have the right to control fertility. Disagreement emerges over the "right" to abortion. Some feminists argue that the argument for a woman's "right" to abortion does not cover all the problems that abortion raises and sets up a problem of conflicting rights: the right of the unborn; the right of the father; the right of the society. Others argue that the "right" exists only when women have become pregnant through an abusive situation such as rape or incest. They maintain, further, that women have a right to abortion if their health or well-being is in danger. While some feminists believe that this right to abortion is absolute, others want some parameters for that right. Some feminists hold that reproductive freedom does not include the right to abortion. These differences among feminists do not necessarily follow the ideological stands of contemporary feminism. They more often arise from differing moral sensibilities. However, feminism asserts as a foundational principle that women must have control over their reproductive capacity.

The universality of this principle reflects the feminist analysis that women are subordinated and discriminated against in all social structures because of their biology and its potential interference with the functioning of social structures, in particular, the political and economic structures of our world. From this analysis, feminism argues that women must be able to control their fertility in order to function freely within these structures. Reproductive freedom is feminism's answer to the subordination and discrimination they experience in patriarchal structures.

But a fundamental question needs to be considered. Is this desire for absolute control over fertility in some ways an implicit acceptance that the male's experience of sexuality without the reality of pregnancy is normative for the human? Feminism denies that its goal is for women to be like men. In fact, feminism has gone to great lengths to develop a variety of feminist alternatives to organizations, style of work, culture, and ritual. But, because of the demands of the social structures framed by male experience, on the question of childbearing, feminism has sought ways to accommodate to those structures rather than to transform them. Is this a fundamental dilemma implicit in contemporary feminism?

Catholic social teaching, while failing to develop an adequate theological anthropology for the human person, female and male, has intuitively been pointing, I suggest, to a profound reality. This intuition is best captured by Paul VI in *Octogesima Adveniens*, where he writes, "Similarly, in many countries a charter for women which could put an end to an actual discrimination and would establish relationships of equality in rights and of respect for their dignity is the object of study and at times of lively demands. We do not have in mind that false equality which would deny the distinctions laid down by the Creator . . . ."[31] Unfortunately Paul VI concludes by speaking of women's "proper role," so the first half of his insight is lost in the dualism of the full statement. However, by insisting on the equal but distinct quality, he is opening the way to explore what that could mean, as well as how it could become structured in social systems.

Can this insight open the way through the dilemma of the dual-nature in Catholic social thought and the dilemma in feminism of women's need to accommodate their childbearing capacity to patriarchal social structures? Would a dialogue between Catholic social thought and feminism reveal that the issue is not women's reproductive capacity; the issue is that the structures are shaped by men's experience and have little or no space for this unique experience of women? It is not women who need to accommodate these structures; these structures need to be transformed to accommodate women. In so changing structures, however, we need to avoid the "separate but equal" concept that worked so well to keep black people subordinate to the dominant society in our history. If the structures did indeed accommodate women's reality, would women then be able to relate more freely to the experience of childbearing and men to the responsibilities and joys of childrearing? An honest exchange between feminism and Catholic social thought could move beyond the limitations of both their dilemmas in search of transformed social structures. The dignity and uniqueness of woman as woman and man as man can be structured into our social systems. It only demands creativity and the political will to open our social structures to the fullness of the human experience.

Common Good. A fundamental principle of Catholic social thought is the recognition of the human person not only as an individual but also as a social being. The dignity of the individual is best realized within the common good of the society. The common good is defined as "the sum total of all those conditions of social living—economic, political, cultural—which make it possible for women and men readily and fully to achieve the perfection of their humanity."[32] This relationship between the individual and the common good in Catholic social teaching is its unique contribution to our understanding of the social order.

Socialist feminism with its image of a social context that sustains women and men economically, politically, socially, and ecologically would find common cause with this particular principle of Catholic social thought. In a feminist revision of Catholic social thought, an equal insistence on the dignity of the human person within the common good stands as a corrective for the socialist tendency to subsume the individual under the society.

Liberal feminism, rooted as it is in liberal doctrine, does not include the common good as an entity. In the liberal tradition, a good society is the sum total of individual goods. A liberal feminist agenda seeks the destruction of patriarchal law that denies both the rights of women as *autonomous adults* and the promotion of individual women within the existing social structures. It does not question whether these existing structures are indeed directed toward the common good. A feminist revision of Catholic social thought would challenge liberal feminism to move beyond the autonomous individual woman to include the context of her society: to move beyond the limited agenda of the promotion of individual women to the wider agenda of seeking a more just society for all.

Feminism, moreover, can point to this principle as a challenge to the church to widen its understanding of the common good in relation to women, as well as women in the relation to the common good. In her article, "New Patterns of Relationship," Margaret Farley points out "from the standpoint of the Roman Catholic ethical tradition, it is a mistake to pit individual good against the good of the community, or the social good, when what is at stake is the fundamental dignity of the individual."[33] This part of the tradition contradicts the very notion of circumscribing women within a particular function or set of duties.

Farley further argues from the point of view of subsidiarity, another principle of Catholic social thought, that the hierarchical model in any social structure must give way to an egalitarian model of social organization if the common good is to be realized. Applying this principle to relationships between women and men, she concludes "it is necessary to argue that in fact the good of the family, church, etc. is better served by a model of leadership which includes collaboration between equals."[34] The twin principles of the common good and subsidiarity demand equality and mutuality not only in personal relations but also in social structures.

Three other themes in Catholic social thought would be enriched by the insights feminism brings: global solidarity, stewardship, and the promotion of peace. Moreover, these feminist agendas would find a strong ally in the social mission of the church as shaped by these themes.

1. Global Solidarity. The catholicity of the church embraces all the peoples of the world. It gives the church the potential to evaluate a situation beyond national or regional interest. It builds upon the unity of the human family and stresses the "mutual obligations to promote the development of all people across the world. . . (insisting that) the structures of the international order must reflect justice."[35]

In Catholic social thought, the global women's movement finds an ally in its challenge to the U.S. women's movement to enlarge its scope and vision in this call for global solidarity. For U.S. feminism to be transformative, it must address not only the dominant patterns in relationships between women and men, but also the relationships between the races, between cultures, and between nation states.

John Paul II in his encyclical *Sollicitudo Rei Socialis* defines solidarity as a "virtue," a "firm and persevering determination to commit oneself to the common good; that is to say, to the good of all and of each individual because we are all really responsible for all."[36] He goes on to speak of the responsibilities of solidarity:

> The exercise of solidarity within each society is valid when its members recognize one another as persons. Those who are more influential because they have a greater share of goods and common services should feel responsible for the weaker and be ready to share with them all they possess. Those who are weaker, for their part, in the same spirit of solidarity, should not adopt a purely passive attitude or one that is destructive of the social fabric, but while claiming their legitimate rights, should do what they can for the good of all. The intermediate groups, in their turn, should not selfishly insist on their particular interests, but respect the interests of others.[37]

There is much in this passage that feminism can appropriate: recognition of the personhood of women; the challenge to women of privilege to respond to the rights of the less privileged; the necessity for the less privileged—the poor, women, people of different races—to claim their legitimate rights.

However, global feminism would challenge that the intermediate groups, as identified by John Paul II, should assume a rather neutral position of respect. The women of the global feminist movement call upon the U.S. women's movement to join them in their struggles not only for personal liberation but also for national and international political and economic justice. Deepening the global feminist perception of the unity and mutuality of all of life further enlarges upon the meaning of solidarity to insist that our very salvation as people is linked. Global feminism identifies links between racism, sexism, and economic and political domination. It understands that racism is not only unjust to people of differing racial and ethnic backgrounds; it destroys the soul of the racist. Sexism is not only unjust to women; it destroys the very soul of the sexist. Economic and political domination is not only unjust to weaker, poorer nations; it is destroying the soul of the powerful nations. Solidarity in the liberation struggles of the peoples is a mutually salvific act.

2. Stewardship. Traditionally, Catholic social thought has used the term *stewardship* when speaking of respect for the earth. The term connotes a kind of ownership of the earth and the necessity to take care of the earth for the future: the call to be good stewards. However, growing ecological and feminist consciousness is beginning to recognize that the human is part of the community of creation, not its owner. Feminism identifies that this shift from a perceived position of dominance over nature to a position of mutuality with the community of creation reflects the primary shift beyond patriarchal thinking, which demands a kind of hierarchy of importance, human over creation, man over woman. This shift in perceiving that we are all mutually linked would enable the human community to understand that its ecologically destructive habits are slowly destroying the very foundation of all life, including the human.

3. Promotion of Peace. Similarly, women's commitment to peace enlarges the understanding of the Catholic social teachings' analysis of the roots of war and dissension. According to Catholic social teaching, "Peace is the fruit of justice and is dependent upon right order among humans and among nations."[38] However, while speaking of the necessity of people being peaceful in their hearts and in their relationships, Catholic social teaching for the most part concentrates on the problems of war between nation states, the possibility of a just war, the morality of deterrence, the immorality of the destruction of innocent non-combatants.

Feminism enters the question from its analysis of patriarchy and seeks to unmask the cultural roots of war. Its analysis of war is shaped by its analytical tool, the "personal is political." According to feminist analysis, the root cause of war is the will to dominate. For radical feminism, the primary root is men's will to dominate women. From this root come all other forms of domination. The will to dominate appears subtly in the patriarchal social structures and the cultural ideology that supports those structures. It appears overtly in all acts of violence: rape, torture, sexual abuse, incest, pornography, domestic violence, the destruction of the earth. It finds its ultimate expression in war, as one nation, usually governed by men, seeks to dominate other nations.

Feminism in particular criticizes militarism, pointing out how the military mind-set is shaped with an emphasis on the domination of the "other," the weak ones, of which women are the primary symbols. It points to the history of women and land being considered the booty of the victorious army. Today it points to the prostitution of women that so commonly accompanies a military presence in a country. Feminism's anger towards militarism and war is deep and abiding.

Furthermore, women traditionally have had to play the role of peacemakers in families. Cultural feminism and radical feminism point to women's experience as having prepared them to be peacemakers. Women are by far the majority in peace movements across the world. But both the planning for war and the negotiations for peace are entirely controlled by men. These negotiations concentrate on the hardware of war rather than on the environment for peace.

Feminism brings a cultural analysis to the problems of militarism and war that would enrich and enlarge Catholic social teaching's perspectives on the meaning and the potential for peace. Without the feminist analysis of the patriarchal roots of violence and war, it is difficult to project that Catholic social teaching will be able to move in that direction.

A feminist revision of Catholic social thought situates the aspirations of the contemporary U.S. women's movement within the larger context of social and global transformation. By including gender analysis in the principal themes of dignity of the human person, economic and political rights, economic justice, option for the poor, the common good, and subsidiarity, women can find in Catholic social ethics a powerful ally in their struggle for liberation. Furthermore, the inclusion of feminist analysis in Catholic social thought enlarges its meaning and understanding of the human experience in social structures.

There are points of disagreement between feminism and Catholic social teaching. Some are apparently irreconcilable, as I have tried to illustrate in this chapter. But I have also tried to show the potential for new insight that a dialogue between feminism and Catholic social theory could generate in our search for a more just world. Because the changes the women's movement have initiated are so profoundly important for the human shape of the future, this dialogue must take place. Moreover, a feminist revision of Catholic social thought would provide Catholic feminists with a perspective from which to bring their voices to the feminist dialogue. It would also challenge the church to clarify and resolve some of its internal contradictions both theoretically and structurally.

Process Questions

1. What would you add to this feminist revision of Catholic social thought? What do you agree with? What do you disagree with?

2. Do you think a feminist revision of Catholic social thought could become an ally for women in their struggle for liberation both in the church and in the society? Why or Why not?

Endnotes

1. *Gaudium Et Spes*, #11 in Joseph Gremillion, ed. *The Gospel Of Peace And Justice* (Maryknoll, NY: Orbis Books, 1976), p. 252. All reference to papal and church documents will be from this source unless otherwise indicated.

2. Carol S. Robb, "A Framework for Feminist Ethics," in *Women's Consciousness, Women's Conscience* (Minneapolis: Winston Press, 1985), p. 211.

3. While church documents are not the only source of Catholic social ethics, they are an identifiable source of teaching and remain the basis for much Catholic social theory and reflection.

4. A brief introduction to Catholic social thought and an outline of the contents of the church documents is available in Peter J. Henriot, Edward P. DeBerri, and Michael J. Schultheis, *Catholic Social Teaching: Our Best Kept Secret*, rev. ed. (Maryknoll, New York: Orbis Books, 1988).

5. For a more detailed account of this shift, see Charles Curran, "The Changing Anthropological Bases of Catholic Social Ethics" in *Moral Theology: A Continuing Journey* (Notre Dame, IN: Notre Dame University Press, 1982), pp. 173-208; and Gremillion, "Evolution of Catholic Social Teaching since Pope John: The Influence of Secular Currents and World Events," in *The Gospel Of Justice And Peace*, pp. 3-124; Christine E. Gudorf, "Major Differences: Liberation Theology and Current Church Teaching" in *Reading In Moral Theology*, No. 5; *Official Catholic Social Teaching*, ed. by Charles E. Curran and Richard A. Mc-

Cormick, SJ (New York: Paulist Press, 1986), pp. 442-457 and Henriot, DeBerri and Schultheis, *Catholic Social Teaching: Our Best Kept Secret*, pp. 7-19.

6. I am indebted to Henriot, Deberri, Schultheis, *Catholic Social Teaching*, pp. 20-22, for this overview of the central themes of Catholic social thought.

7. Curran, *Moral Theology: A Continuing Journey*, p. 176.

8. *Quadragesimo Anno*, #71 (Washington, DC: National Catholic Welfare Conference, 1942), p. 27. The publishing organization is now called the United States Catholic Conference.

9. See "The Juridical Status of Women in Contemporary Ecclesial Law," by Francis Morrisey, OMI, in *Sexism And Church Law*, ed. by James Coriden (New York: Paulist Press, 1977), p. 2. Morrisey writes, "The Code legislation, as it stood in 1917, certainly ascribed a subordinate status for women, who were considered almost dependent, passive or inferior members in the Church." The new code of canon has attempted to correct some of this bias.

10. *Pacem In Terris*, #s 39-43.

11. *Pacem In Terris*, #41.

12. *Gaudium Et Spes*, #29.

13. *Gaudium Et Spes*, #23.

14. *Gaudium Et Spes*, #8.

15. *Gaudium Et Spes*, #s 55 and 60.

16. *Octogesima Adveniens*, #13.

17. *Justice In The World*, #s 41-46.

18. *Justice In The World*, #14.

19. *Justice In The World*, #16.

20. *Laborem Exercens*, #19, *Origins* 11:15 (September 24, 1981).

21. *Puebla Document*, #834 in *Puebla And Beyond*, ed. by John Eagleson and Philip Scharper (Maryknoll, NY: Orbis Press, 1979), p. 233.

22. *Puebla Document* #s 835-840.

23. *Puebla Document* #s 841, 846-848.

24. *Economic Justice For All: Catholic Social Teaching And The U.S. Economy*,#207 *Origins*, 16:24 (November 27, 1986).

25. *Sollicitudo Rei Socialis*, #14 in *Origins* 17:38 (March 3, 1988), p. 646.

26. Curran, *Moral Theology: A Continuing Journey*, p. 35.

27. Henriot, DeBerri and Schultheis, p. 18.

28. "LCWR Board Urges Change of Course," *Origins*, 14:40 (March 21, 1985), p. 655.

29. The term "feminization of poverty" identifies the trend of growing poverty among women of all ages in the U.S. It was first identified in 1978 by Diana Pearce in "Feminization of Poverty: Women, Work and Welfare," *Urban Social Change Review*, Feb. 1978 and reiterated in the Final Report of the National Advisory Council on Economic Opportunity (Washington, DC: U.S. Government Printing Office, 1981).

30. Rosalind Pollack Petchesky, "Reproductive Freedom: Beyond 'A Woman's Right To Choose,' " *Signs: Journal Of Women In Culture And Society*, V:4 (Summer, 1980), pp. 669-670. See also Jaggar, pp. 319-320.

31. *Octogesima Adveniens*, #13.

32. Henriot, DeBerri, and Schultheis, p. 21.

33. Margaret Farley, "New Patterns of Relationship" in *Woman: New Dimensions*, ed. by Walter Burghardt, SJ (New York: Paulist Press, 1977), p. 68.

34. Farley, p. 69.
35. Henriot, DeBerri, and Schultheis, p. 22.
36. *Sollicitudo Rei Socialis,* #38.
37. *Sollicitudo Rei Socialis,* #39.
38. Henriot, DeBerri, and Schultheis, p. 22.

5

The Real Revolution

The decision to feed the world
is the real decision. No revolution
has chosen it. For that choice requires
that women shall be free.
  —Adrienne Rich[1]

"It was the best of times, it was the worst of times . . . ." So Charles Dickens characterized the French Revolution. Throughout history people have been prone to see their age as the worst and the best, but that insight is particularly apt for our age because our potential for destruction is so great. Daily we become more and more aware of the ecological destruction all around us. There continue to be wars and rumors of wars: Northern Ireland, the Middle East, the Horn of Africa, Angola, Namibia, Mozambique, Central America, the Philippines. Violence and terrorism stalk our skies, our city streets, and even our homes. Debt looms like a vulture over our economies and our abilities to care for our peoples. Political and economic apartheid paralyses our spirit. Hunger, starvation, disease, drugs, homelessness, and despair stare out from our newspapers and TV screens. Militarism grows like a cancer all over the world. Refugees roam the earth seeking a home. And the children—poor, hungry, hopeless, terrorized, brutalized, and abandoned. The suffering of the earth and the human family is too great to bear.

But these are also the best of times, for groups of people everywhere are beginning to realize just how endangered we are. We can point to the growing ecological movement, the peace movements, liberation movements, and the women's movement. There is promise that an appropriate use of technology will enable us to break through some of the overwhelming problems that confront us. Among some world leaders there seems to be emerging a renewed political will to look beyond ideologies and narrow national interest toward a quest for the well-being of earth and all its peoples. There is a growing realization that we must seek creative and dramatic responses to the devastation that surrounds us. The signs of hope are fragile, but they are among us.

In this book, I have been addressing one of the signs of hope—the women's movement and its search for a more just world. Feminist analysis points to a fundamental cause of the problems we face: the will to dominate and control. Feminists identify that will to dominate as central to the patriarchal culture. Feminism points to many forms that dominating relationships take. For example, the relationships between men and women, the rich and the poor, powerful cultures and weak cultures, the so-called developed world and the developing world, the strong and the weak, the human and the earth. Feminism challenges these relationships to move beyond domination and subordination to mutuality and inclusiveness. But for that transformation to take place, changes must be initiated in many dimensions of our lives. In this concluding chapter, I will reflect on several arenas demanding change: culture, attitudes, and structures. My efforts to develop a feminist-revised Catholic social ethic shapes the direction of these reflections. My remarks are primarily referring to the U.S., but can be applicable wherever appropriate.

Cultural Change

A society's value system is at the heart of its culture. Religion which is at the core of culture functions to legitimate that value system. Cultural values also direct a society to identify and reward what it considers meaningful and to disregard what it does not value. Feminism has identified the patriarchal core of most cultures and how the religious dimensions within them legitimate those values.

If we are to move beyond our present destructive mode, that patriarchal core must be transformed. As radical feminist analysis has illustrated, patriarchal culture, built on a structure of domination and subordination, is by its very nature violent: overtly violent are such acts as rape, pornography, woman-battering, torture, war, ecological destruction; and covertly violent are such acts as exclusion, psychological diminishment, detached rationality, economic dependency, imposed limitations and political control.[2] By it very nature and structure, patriarchy demands hierarchy. If one group is to dominate, then perforce there must be others to be dominated. Throughout this book, I have given innumerable examples of one group assuming superiority over another: men over women, human over nature, the white race over all others, the rich over the poor. I would like to note, however, that in talking about patriarchal culture, I am not talking about individual men and women. We are all, women and men, infected with patriarchal values, because it is the primary cultural ambiance of our church and our world.

Central to moving beyond our patriarchal culture is the re-valuing of the human person. The masculine can no longer be the defining sex, whose experience gives shape to our social structures, our ecclesial structures, and our structures of knowledge and value. Nor can the Western, caucasian, industrialized society be the model for the rest of the world. We already are suffering the failures of that model, for example, in the growing destruction of our environments, the increasing number of people in desperate poverty, the high incidence of abortion, the ineptness of our educational systems, and the drug epidemic with its daily violence.

To re-value the individual person sounds so obvious as to appear trite. But our social attitudes and structures, in fact, do not support the dignity of each person, as the continuing struggle of so many people to achieve human dignity testifies. Their very struggles point to the need for the transformation of social structures, if the rhetoric of the dignity of the human person is to have any meaning.

Structural Change

The idea of structural change is often paralyzing to think about and could lead to apathy or despair. Yet, history is the record of structural changes from pre-historic, through ancient, medieval, renaissance, and modern times. The question for us is whether we choose to be simply observers of our historical moments, or whether we choose to use our life and energy to be subjects of our time, to work actively to create the future.

To be active subjects of the future demands a vision and hope for what that future will be. A feminist-revised Catholic social ethic is one of those visions. What concrete objectives does it offer for re-thinking the shape of our political, economic, and social structures?

Political Structures: Political structures identify how power is organized within a society or a group. An alternative approach to the patriarchal structures of domination and hierarchy is to develop structures of mutuality and participation. The goal is to transform attitudes and structures from power over (hierarchy) to empowerment of individuals and people, a kind of political process that supports the dignity of the individual. Structures must be designed to insure people meaningful, effective participation in the decisions that shape their lives.

Participatory structures do not deny the exercise of legitimate leadership nor do they deny legitimate divisions of labor. They do resist the tendency to define one kind of labor and those who engage in it as superior to other kinds of labor and whose who engage in them. Built into participatory structures are a deep and abiding reverence for the common good and the value of the myriad kinds of work required to support the common good. The contribution of each person is valued for what she/he brings to the common good.

The principle of subsidiarity is fundamental to participatory political structures. Subsidiarity means that "responsibilities and decisions should be attended to as closely as possible to the level of individual initiative in local communities and institutions. Mediating structures of families, neighborhood, community groups, small businesses, and local governments should be fostered and participated in. But larger government structures do have a role when greater social coordination and regulation are necessary for the common good."[3] Subsidiarity creates the needed balance between the individual and the common good, so that neither takes precedence over the other. The individual good is not ignored in pursuit of the common good, nor is the common good ignored in the pursuit of individual advancement.

The current trend toward a mass society that we experience in our daily lives militates against meaningful participatory structures. However, the technological revolution in communications offers creative opportunities to develop structures of participation. What we need is the vision and political will to use modern technology to liberate rather than to anaesthetize, consumerize, and package our lives. That decision, of course, points to the cultural transformation demanded by our times.

Economic Structures: Economic structures reflect political and cultural structures. The wealthy are the powerful; the powerful usually wield power in order to maintain their control both in the political and the economic structures. They assume a position of superiority over others and demand subordination. As a society we give them a kind of honor and reverence their personal conduct often does not deserve. Note, for example, our fascination with the superstars in the financial, political, and entertainment worlds, even when these personalities are destructive of some of our most cherished values, such as integrity, democracy, fairness, family life, religion.

Transformation toward more just economic structures will demand a more equitable distribution of both power and resources. A full description of that restructuring is beyond the scope of this book, so I will speak to only one issue which is fundamental to that restructuring for women.

From a feminist analysis one dimension of this restructuring will necessitate the recognition of the equal and mutual value of both the reproductive domestic work and the productive work in the society. It will mean moving beyond the patriarchal division of labor that identifies man as the economic agent and head of the family, and woman as the economically dependent "heart" of the family. It will recognize the mutual responsibility of both women and men for both the reproduction and the production of society.

Structurally, this change will open up work structures to accommodate women's unique experience of childbearing and men's responsibility in childrearing. These changes are already beginning to shape our work worlds as companies initiate policies of maternity/paternity leave, flex-time and shared time. They are also apparent in the growing number of parents who are sharing the work of parenting. These changes are resulting from the changing population of the work force, changing economic conditions, and changing expectations of both women and men. However, such changes will remain cosmetic and pragmatic until we shift beyond the deeply entrenched patriarchal attitudes about the "proper" roles of women and men to a culture which appreciates and supports the unique potential of each person.

Economic independence is an essential dimension of women's full participation in all structures of society. In reality, for most women and men, this economic independence will translate into an economic co-dependence for the family, recognizing the economic contribution not only of productive work but also of domestic reproductive work. This change will lay the groundwork for women and men to recognize and appreciate their economic interdependence and mutuality in responsibility for the quality of family life and the care of the young and the old. Decisions on tasks to be fulfilled in both the family and the work place can then be mutually determined rather than pre-determined by some kind of role expectation.

Social Structures: Fundamental to any changes in political and economic structures is a change in our social structures—how we relate to one another. Social restructuring will demand new patterns of relationships that are non-coercive and non-violent. Obviously, such restructuring requires the end of any kind of culture built on domination.

Rather than structures of social control and conditioning demanded by the culture of patriarchy, such as current gender formation and role determination, we will need to develop structures of mutuality and solidarity. Often we think of such values as only attitudinal, but they are attitudes which can be structured into how we relate to one another. Such restructuring illustrates how integrally connected social relationships are with political structures. Social relationships built on superior-inferior models reflect political and economic structures of power to control as, for example, the history of racism in the U.S. illustrates. The "personal is political."

One example of how some groups have worked to move beyond hierarchal structures to structures of mutuality and solidarity is the renewal process of many religious communities of women. The Second Vatican Council first called upon religious communities to renew their lives and look to the charism of their founders. While the external signs of renewal are most obvious to the casual observer, such as contemporary dress and greater freedom in the choice of work and living, the most profound transformation for many communities has been in the restructuring of internal relationships. They have moved from a hierarchical model with a "Mother Superior," a particularly inappropriate model for a community of committed adults, to models of collegiality and subsidiarity. Moreover, they have created structures of collegiality that develop mutuality and solidarity among the members as they seek to honor individual charisms as well as the common good. In so doing many communities have found themselves under the scrutiny of the Vatican, which despite the language of its social teaching, operates out of a patriarchal, hierarchal structure. These attempts are indeed laboratories for the future and show promise that with the political will, changes can occur.

Moreover, as I have continued to point out through this text, within a feminist-revised Catholic social ethic, the challenge to develop structures of mutuality and solidarity is not only directed toward women and men. It is directed to all dimensions of our life on the planet: between races, nations, cultures, and between humans and the earth.

All Is Connected

All social structures mutually inform each other. Cultural values direct social, political, and economic values while these values are at the heart of what we value as a culture. We separate these structures for the purpose of analysis, but in seeking strategic means to move toward transformation we need to understand how our social structures are woven together into the pattern of our lives. At first the very coherence of the system makes it appear unmovable. However, its very coherence also means that a change in one dimension of a culture perforce demands a change in all other dimensions. The movement of women in the society is illustrating that reality.

Any process of change or transformation is multi-dimensional and, therefore, possible strategies for change must be multi-dimensional. Within the social structures of education and family, a consistent introduction of the affirmation of human dignity, the equality of all persons, especially women and men, is essential to cultural change. It also demands that we challenge the cultural, racial, class, and gender stereotypes the media beam into our living rooms.

Critical to this cultural transformation is the necessity for the religious traditions and their supporting institutions to recognize and repudiate the inherent sexism and patriarchy that shape images of God, sacred writings, language, doctrinal pronouncements, institutional forms, and the choice of leaders. Religious patriarchy has legitimated social, political, and economic patriarchy throughout the ages. The Catholic church must judge it actions according to its own teachings. The fundamentals of Catholic social teaching demand that the church eliminate its own sexism and patriarchy if it indeed is going to be able to be a positive voice in the shaping of the non-patriarchal future.

Working for new political processes and structures which guarantee people participation in the decisions that effect their lives at all levels is essential to the task of political transformation facing us. These processes and structures need to be introduced in the workplace, in community groups, and in all gatherings of the human community, as well as in the more formal political structures that govern cities, nation states, and the world.

Economic equity demands major re-thinking and restructuring of our use of the earth's resources so they are available more equitably to all peoples. It also demands a reverence for the community of creation of which we are a member. Part of that transformation will occur with a political restructuring of our use of power. In analyzing all our social structures we continually need to assess who decides, who benefits, and who pays.

Fundamental to all social change is transformation beyond patriarchy. The clear message of the results of the International Decade for Women 1975-1985 is that the movement of so many women beyond poverty, dependence, and violence is contingent upon the evolution of societies beyond the current imbalances of economic and political power that shape our world. But concomitantly, a society's ability to move toward justice for all is contingent upon the liberation of women. Transformation beyond our current modes of destruction demands the end of the patriarchal culture. That will be the beginning of the real revolution.

The decision to feed the world
is the real decision. No revolution
has chosen it. For that choice requires
that women shall be free.

—Adrienne Rich

Endnotes

1. Adrienne Rich, "Hunger," in *The Dream Of A Common Language* (New York: W.W. Norton, Inc., 1978), p. 13.

2. See Chapter 3, pp. 55ff.

3. Peter J. Henriot, Edward P. DeBerri, and Michael J. Schultheis, *Catholic Social Teaching: Our Best Kept Secret,* res. ed. (Maryknoll, NY: Orbis Press, 1988), p. 21.

Appendix A: The Women's Movement—1963-1989

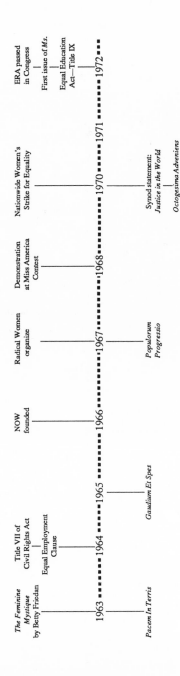

Appendix A: The Women's Movement—1963-1989 (continued)

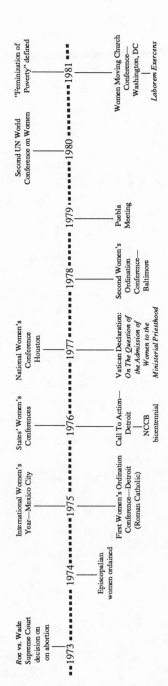

Appendix A: The Women's Movement—1963-1989 (continued)

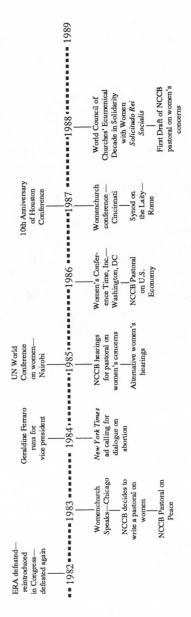

1982 ERA defeated—reintroduced in Congress—defeated again

Womenchurch Speaks—Chicago

NCCB decides to write a pastoral on women

NCCB Pastoral on Peace

1983

1984 Geraldine Ferraro runs for vice president

New York Times ad calling for dialogue on abortion

1985 UN World Conference on women—Nairobi

NCCB hearings for pastoral on women's concerns

Alternative women's hearings

1986 Women's Conference Time, Inc.—Washington, DC

NCCB Pastoral on U.S. Economy

1987 10th Anniversary of Houston Conference

Womenchurch conference—Cincinnati

Synod on the Laity—Rome

1988 World Council of Churches' Ecumenical Decade in Solidarity with Women

Solicitudo Rei Socialis

First Draft of NCCB pastoral on women's concerns

1989

Appendix B: Ideological and Historical Strands of Contemporary Feminism

Primary Carriers:
Bureaucratic and
Organizational Feminists

Primary Carriers:
Diffused Through
the Movement

LIBERAL

—Political/Legal Analysis

—Equal Rights and
Opportunities Before
the Law

CULTURAL

—Affirmation of
Women's Moral Power

—Diffusion of Women's
Moral Vision
Throughout Society

WOMEN'S LIBERATION

—Political/Legal
—Economic
—Social
—Cultural

RADICAL

—Analysis of the
Culture of Patriarchy

—Creation of an
Alternative Feminist
Future

Primary Carriers:
Collectivists' Groups

SOCIALIST

—Economic Analysis of
Reproduction and
Production
—Economic Independence
—Reproduction
Freedom

Primary Carriers:
Collectivists' Groups